CONTENTS

I love sports. I always have and I always will. You probably do too, or you wouldn't be on this journey with my son Jonathan and me.

What I love about sports is the competition. Not only with the other team or your opponent across the court, but also the competition with yourself. Each time you're on the field of play, whether at practice or in a match, you're stretching yourself, trying to become a better athlete.

As a pastor and having served as chaplain for the Dallas Cowboys and the Dallas Mavericks, I've found some striking parallels between sports and the kingdom of God. I'm not the first to see these parallels, however. The apostle Paul referred to sports several times as a way to explain how a Christian should "run with endurance the race that is set before us" in order to win the trophy—or in their case, the laurel wreath.

Here are some examples:

Do you not know that those who run in a race all run, but only one receives the prize? Run in such a way that you may win. Everyone who competes in the games exercises self-control in all things. They then do it to receive a perishable wreath, but we an imperishable. Therefore I run in such a way, as not without aim; I box in such a way, as not beating the air; but I discipline my body and make it my slave, so that, after I have preached to others, I myself will not be disqualified (1 Corinthians 9:24-27).

I press on toward the goal for the prize of the upward call of God in Christ Jesus (Philippians 3:14).

Discipline yourself for the purpose of godliness; for bodily discipline is only of little profit, but godliness is profitable for all things, since it holds promise for the present life and also for the life to come (1 Timothy 4:7-8).

If anyone competes as an athlete, he does not win the prize unless he competes according to the rules (2 Timothy 2:5).

I have fought the good fight, I have finished the course, I have kept the faith; in the future there is laid up for me the crown of righteousness, which the Lord, the righteous Judge, will award to me on that day; and not only to me, but also to all who have loved His appearing (2 Timothy 4:7-8).

Since we have so great a cloud of witnesses surrounding us, let us also lay aside every encumbrance and the sin which so easily entangles us, and let us run with endurance the race that is set before us, fixing our eyes on Jesus, the author and perfecter of faith, who for the joy set before Him endured the cross, despising the shame, and has sat down at the right hand of the throne of God (Hebrews 12:1-2).

You'll notice that in these sports analogies, Paul talks a lot about training or fighting or pressing on. As an athlete, that's something you already know. The more you train, the better you perform on the field. The more you work out consistently in the weight room, the stronger you become.

You probably also already know that patience is required. Patience is key both on the field and in our Christian life.

You're on the right track by reading this book and by having a coach or mentor or parent who will help guide you through the content in this book. To gain the full advantage, I want you to consider the questions, exercises, and information presented on these pages as though you're preparing for a game. In a way, that's what it is. Some people call it the "game of life" and for our purposes, that's a good analogy. Just know that this game is far more crucial than any game you'll play on the field. If you lose a match against a worthy opponent, you can always play another day. But the game of life happens only once. You have one shot at winning. And I'm confident you will win if you make it your goal to be God's masterpiece in your body, mind, and soul.

As you go through the book, I'll stop in every few pages with one of my Here to Help insights. My son Jonathan will add some valuable information in his Game On with Jonathan sidebars.

Jonathan and I both know you love sports as much as we do. Our hope is that you'll also love and value the life God has given you. That you'll turn your focus on the game that really counts and learn to excel at life. We don't want you to miss out on anything God has for you.

Be the masterpiece God created you to be—on and off the field.

> **Are you a parent or coach who wants to go through this with your student athlete? Download the leader's guide at go.tonyevans.org/coach.**

THE
PLAYBOOK

LEVEL I

MY FORM

KINGDOM KEY 1

IDENTITY

You will learn how to see yourself as God sees you.

You will discover your own personality style as well as how to identify the style of others.

You will create your own personal brand.

WORD SKETCH:

Unique
very special, distinctively characteristic, being without a like

Rare
marked by unusual quality or appeal, seldom occurring

Valuable
of great use and importance

The distinguishing qualities of a person that make that person rare, unique, and valuable.

Origin of IDENTITY: Middle French identité

First Known Use: 1570

RULE BOOK

[God] creates each of us by Christ Jesus to join Him in the work He does, the good work He has ready for us to do, work we had better be doing. Ephesians 2:10

But you are the ones chosen by God, chosen for the high calling of priestly work, chosen to be a holy people, God's instruments to do his work and speak out for him. 1 Peter 2:9

___TRANSCRIBE
WRITE IN YOUR OWN WORDS

TRANSLATE___
WHAT DOES IT MEAN?

When Cliff Young showed up at the start line of the 1983 Sydney to Melbourne Ultramarathon, everyone assumed the 61 year old farmer dressed in overalls and boots was a spectator. They were amazed when he picked up a race number.

This particular marathon was 543 miles long and took about 7 days for athletes in their 20's and 30's to complete. Cliff was obviously no athlete in his prime. Who he was was a sheep farmer. Because his family couldn't afford horses, he had spent much of his life running sheep over the 2,000 acre farm whenever storms came in. With 2,000 sheep spread across all that space, it would often take him three days to chase them all. To him, this race seemed like just a small extension of what he spent his life doing.

For the first days of the race, Cliff's shuffling gate kept him well behind the leaders. But, while the rest of the runners would sleep at night, Cliff continued onward. By the final evening, he was in first place. He ended up not only winning the race, but beating the record time by nine hours. His unique shuffle running style is still used by runners to this day.

Knowing your identity means understanding where you've come from, your strengths, and your weaknesses. When you truly understand that, you can begin to see past the labels the world puts on you. Cliff Young didn't think he was an elite athlete. He was a sheep farmer, and he was a good one. He knew his abilities and decided to apply them in ways the world didn't necessarily expect.

Your identity comes from a Creator that knows no limits. When you begin to examine your identity through His eyes and not earthly labels, you may be surprised to find what you're made of.

You can read more about this story online by visiting us here:

go.tonyevans.org/athletes

JUST FOR FUN

When a company develops a marketing campaign around their product, they come up with several key components such as:

A. Logo
B. Tagline
C. Vision statement

Spend some time drawing your own personal logo. Make sure it reflects who you are as a person—strong, quiet, solid, aggressive, etc.

After your logo, develop a tagline that lets others know who you are in a simple yet creative statement.

Sample taglines:

Nike: **Just Do It**	Milk: **Got Milk?**
Apple: **Think Different**	M&M's: **Melts in your mouth, not in your hands**
McDonalds: **I'm Lovin' It**	The Urban Alternative: **Teaching Truth, Transforming Lives**

Finally, draft a vision statement that sets the tone and direction for where you want to head in your life and what you want to represent to others.

Sample vision statements:

Goodwill: Every person has the opportunity to achieve his/her fullest potential and participate in and contribute to all aspects of life.

Habitat for Humanity: A world where everyone has a decent place to live.

Focus on the Family: Redeemed families, communities, and societies worldwide through Christ.

World Vision: For every child, life in all its fullness; Our prayer for every heart, the will to make it so.

HERE TO HELP with Tony Evans

Admit it. Have you ever gone to the kitchen after a batch of cookies or a cake was put in the oven and licked out the bowl? Or have you ever grabbed the spatula from your brother or sister before they could lick it first? Or how about just opening up a ready-made cookie roll before it bakes and eating a spoonful or two?

Most people love cookie dough. They love it so much that manufacturers now stick it in ice cream and milk shakes.

But have you ever been tempted to rush to the bowl when the eggs and salt were being mixed together? Probably not. Or have you ever wanted to grab the baking soda and dump a spoonful into your mouth? What about the butter Have you ever snuck into the kitchen after everyone has gone to sleep to swipe a stick of butter? O quietly lifted the lid off of the flour container so that no one heard and you didn't get caught getting a spoon to eat?

I doubt it. Because none of those things on their own are all that good. Butter by itself tastes nasty Baking soda by itself is bitter. Flour by itself tastes dry. Eggs by themselves are disgusting. In fact, som people think they are disgusting even when they've been cooked.

None of those ingredients by themselves would be enough to tempt your tastebuds, right?

Yet when someone steps into the kitchen and mixes them all together toward an intended purpose they are really good. Stick them in the oven over some heat and you better watch out because the tray is now the most sought-after thing in the whole house. It's priceless.

Just like you.

You are a unique mixture of your history, background, gifts, skills, passions, vision, talent, personality experiences, genetics, and more. Sure, some of those things might have been bitter on their owr Maybe you've had some hard times. Some of those things may seem dry; you may not know yet who your vision or gifts are. Some of those things—on their own—may not make sense to you right now. Bu the great thing about God is that He has a way of mixing everything together and turning them int a priceless and unique YOU.

Your identity is who you are. You are not just a head. You are not just arms. You are not just you thoughts. If you built a character for a video game and didn't include all of the pieces of the bod you would have a zombie, right? When you choose your form to play in a game, you have to in clude all of the pieces before you can move to the next level. Your identity form is made up of som things that might have been bitter; they might even have been painful. But God teaches us lessor and makes us stronger through these times if we will let Him. There are probably also successes an strengths in your identity, but sometimes you might forget to include them when you view yourse Maybe you are focusing too much on what is wrong. But a healthy identity form recognizes th strength of the person. You have strengths. Maybe you are good with blocking, good with peopl or good in sports. Whatever it is, don't forget to include the strengths of your identity form as well.

Grow from the pain and weaknesses. Maximize and feed the strengths. Allow for your uniquenes When you do all of that, God will mix it all together so you will have a strong identity form to mov to the next level well.

Tony Evans

each question, circle the letter by the answer that best reflects the way you think and feel.

am confident that I was created on purpose and for a purpose.

Ⓐ Always   **Ⓑ** Most of the time   **Ⓒ** Sometimes   **Ⓓ** No, I am not sure

am proud of my name.

Ⓐ Always   **Ⓑ** Most of the time   **Ⓒ** Seldom   **Ⓓ** Never

base the way I feel about myself on my performance in school, in sports, or another activity.

Ⓐ Always   **Ⓑ** Most of the time   **Ⓒ** Seldom   **Ⓓ** Never

ometimes I feel worthless because I'm not very good at anything.

Ⓐ Always   **Ⓑ** Most of the time   **Ⓒ** Seldom   **Ⓓ** Never

My parents or other adults in my life make it clear that I am important to them.

Ⓐ Always   **Ⓑ** Most of the time   **Ⓒ** Seldom   **Ⓓ** Never

am comfortable being myself around people who are different from me.

Ⓐ Always   **Ⓑ** Most of the time   **Ⓒ** Seldom   **Ⓓ** Never

would never pick a hairstyle, clothes, or shoes that my friends didn't approve of first.

Ⓐ I always get their opinion first   **Ⓑ** I might if I thought they would approve   **Ⓒ** Only if it was something weird   **Ⓓ** My friends let me be me

can comfortably discuss my strengths and weaknesses.

Ⓐ Yes, with most people   **Ⓑ** Yes, with some people   **Ⓒ** Not really   **Ⓓ** What strengths and weaknesses?

think most people would reject me if they knew the real me.

Ⓐ Always   **Ⓑ** Most of the time   **Ⓒ** Seldom   **Ⓓ** Never

I sometimes wonder what will happen to me when I die.

Ⓐ Always   **Ⓑ** Most of the time   **Ⓒ** Seldom   **Ⓓ** Never

ENTITY SCORE CARD

				POINT TOTAL						POINT TOTAL
A-5	B-4	C-3	D-2		6.	A-5	B-4	C-3	D-2	
A-5	B-4	C-3	D-2		7.	A-2	B-3	C-4	D-5	
A-2	B-3	C-4	D-5		8.	A-5	B-4	C-3	D-2	
A-2	B-3	C-4	D-5		9.	A-2	B-3	C-4	D-5	
A-5	B-4	C-3	D-2		10.	A-2	B-3	C-4	D-5	

TOTAL POINTS

Results on the next page

If your score was:

40-50: You are evidently secure in your identity and have a good support system of family and friends who have equipped you to know that you were created by God on purpose and that you have a purpose in life. You may enjoy hobbies and activities, but you are not defined by what you do or what you are good at. You are aware that if Jesus Christ is your Savior, your eternity is secure in Him.

30-39: You might want to take some time to consider yourself as a human being rather than a human doing. When we identify ourselves by what we do instead of who God made us to be, we run the risk of having an identity crisis when we can no longer do the things we once did. The Bible tells us in Matthew 7:15 that we are known by our "fruit"—not only by what we do with our lives, but by how we show forth God's love and nature.

20-29: It's never too late to understand that you can have an identity that is secure in the Rock of Jesus Christ Who loves you unconditionally, Who never changes, and Who will never forsake you or leave you alone. He invites all people to come to Him just as they are. God has given each of us gifts and made each of us uniquely and wonderfully. By spending time worshipping Him and learning His Word, we can learn what our gifts are and the purpose He has for our lives.

In each of the following categories, circle any or all that apply to you.

LION

Takes charge	Bold
Determined	Purposeful
Assertive	Decision maker
Firm	Leader
Enterprising	Goal-driven
Competitive	Self-reliant
Enjoys challenges	Adventurous

DOUBLE THE
NUMBER CIRCLED

OTTER

Takes risks	Fun-loving
Visionary	Likes variety
Motivator	Enjoys change
Energetic	Creative
Very verbal	Group-oriented
Promoter	Mixes easily
Avoids details	Optimistic

DOUBLE THE
NUMBER CIRCLED

GOLDEN RETRIEVER

Loyal	Adaptable
Non-demanding	Sympathetic
Even-keeled	Thoughtful
Avoids conflict	Nurturing
Enjoys routine	Patient
Dislikes change	Tolerant
Deep relationships	Good listener

DOUBLE THE
NUMBER CIRCLED

BEAVER

Deliberate	Discerning
Controlled	Detailed
Reserved	Analytical
Predictable	Inquisitive
Practical	Precise
Orderly	Persistent
Factual	Scheduled

DOUBLE THE NUMBER CIRCLED

STRENGTHS ASSESSMENT CHART

Take the final score from each trait box and plot the number in the corresponding grid boxes below. Now you can see the level of each personality-strength cluster you have and in what proportion. Following the chart is a description of each personality strength cluster.

	LION	OTTER	GOLDEN RETRIEVER	BEAVER
30				
15				
0				

LION

This personality likes to lead. The lion is good at making decisions and is very goal-oriented. They enjoy challenges, difficult assignments, and opportunity for advancement. Because lions are thinking of the goal, they can step on people to reach it. Lions can be very aggressive and competitive. Lions must learn not to be too bossy or to take charge in other's affairs.

- Strength: Goal-oriented, strong, direct
- Weakness: Argumentative, too dictatorial
- Limitation: Doesn't understand that directness can hurt others, hard time expressing

OTTER

Otters are very social creatures. Otter personalities love people. They enjoys being popular and influencing and motivating others. Otters can sometimes be hurt when people do not like them. Otter personalities usually have lots of friends, but not deep relationships. They love to goof-off. (They are notorious for messy rooms.) Otters like to hurry and finish jobs. (Jobs are not often done well.)

- Strength: People person, open, positive
- Weakness: Talks too much, too permissive
- Limitation: Remembering past commitments, follow through with discipline

GOLDEN RETRIEVER

Good at making friends. Very loyal. Retriever personalities do not like big changes. They look for security. Can be very sensitive. Very caring. Has deep relationships, but usually only a couple of close friends. Wants to be loved by everyone. Looks for appreciation. Works best in a limited situation with a steady work pattern.

- Strength: Accommodating, calm, affirming
- Weakness: Indecisive, indifferent, unable to express emotions, too soft on other people
- Limitation: Seeing the need to be more assertive, holding others accountable

BEAVER

Beavers think that there is a right way to do everything and they want to do it exactly that way. Beaver personalities are very creative. They desire to solve everything. Desire to take their time and do it right. Beavers do not like sudden changes. They need reassurance.

- Strength: High standards, order, respect
- Weakness: Unrealistic expectations of self and others, too perfect
- Limitation: Seeing the optimistic side of things, expressing flexibility

The 400 meter sprint in track and field is one of the most grueling races in a track meet. This long sprint has a way of taking everything out of you while still demanding that you end up strong across the finish line. The most important thing to any 400 meter sprinter in the midst of a race is his or her form. They need to be very cautious about making sure that everything is perfectly aligned as they run—from the top of their head to the bottom of their feet. However, the reality of this particular race is that it is sure to challenge perfect form. The identity of a runner's form is put to the test in the last 150 meters as extreme fatigue sets in. Therefore, success in the 400 meter is directly tied to the one who holds true to their form the strongest and the longest, to the one who does not allow the reality of fatigue to break down the identity of their form. In other words, this race will not be given to the swift but to the one who endures to the end.

Many aspects of running the race of life can be extremely grueling. There are so many things that can hit you from so many directions that can cause the identity of your form in Christ to begin the breakdown. Just like the 400 meter, it holds true that those who are successful in the race of life build a solid identity of faith and stand firm in that form in the midst of their fatigue. First you must understand and build your form, which is your identity. Secondly, once you understand and have built your identity, you must function in it without allowing circumstances to break it down. Building your form and holding true to its identity is the key to a successful life.

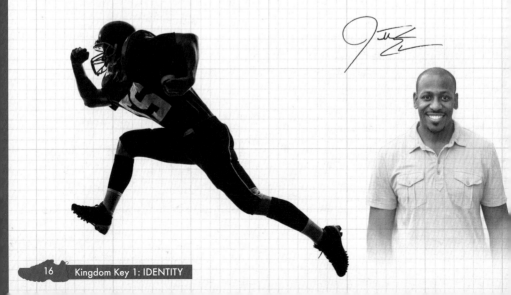

KINGDOM KEY 2

INTEGRITY

OBJECTIVES:

1. You will discover how integrity relates to different areas of life.

2. You will see how you rate yourself on integrity.

3. You will read about consequences related to a lack of integrity.

Honest
free from deception,
speaking and living the truth

Decent
well-formed, marked by
a right heart and actions

Complete
not limited or lacking
in any necessary area

WORD SKETC

Seeking to live honestly and right; complete

Origin of INTEGRITY: Middle English *integrit*
First Known Use: 14th century

RULE BOOK

Don't indulge your ego at the expense of your soul. Live an exemplary life...so that your actions will refute their prejudices. Then they'll be won over to God's side.
1 Peter 2:12

I'd say you'll do best by filling your minds and meditating on things true, noble, reputable, authentic, compelling, gracious—the best, not the worst; the beautiful, not the ugly; things to praise, not things to curse. Put into practice what you learned from me, what you heard and saw and realized. Do that, and God, who makes everything work together, will work you into his most excellent harmonies.
Philippians 4:8

May integrity and uprightness preserve me, for I wait for you.
Psalm 25:21 (ESV)

___TRANSCRIBE

WRITE IN YOUR OWN WORDS

TRANSLATE___

WHAT DOES IT MEAN?

JUST FOR FUN

The integrity of the game can be looked at as the sidelines or boundaries of the field. It is an unmovable standard by which all activity should be pursued and accomplished. Once the boundaries are crossed there is an automatic penalty that will ensue.

Puck or quarter slide Game:

Have a quarter or something solid that will easily slide across the table. Each person will take a turn sliding the puck or quarter toward someone else that is sitting across from them. The goal, is to play the game without breaking the integrity of the table. That is, slide it as close to the edge as possible without the quarter or solid object falling off. The closer you get to the edge of the table without falling off gives you a point. If the puck is hanging off the edge of the table but does not fall over you get two points. However, if you slide the puck or solid object too far and it breaks the integrity of the table you are out of the game. The goal is to play hard without breaking the table integrity. The first one to 10 wins.

The goal in life is to live it to the fullest, play to the fullest, and experience the fullness of what life has to offer. However, you must stay within the boundaries in order to have a full experience of success.

HERE TO HELP with Tony Evans

Have you ever seen a building implode on itself? One second you are looking at a fully standing building, bridge, or tunnel and within seconds, the entire thing turns into a pile of ashes and debris.

In the controlled demolition industry, a number of small explosives are placed strategically throughout the structure. They are then detonated within a set and quick time frame so that the structure's integrity is removed and it collapses on itself nearly at the rate of freefall.

Wikipedia: "Structural integrity is a performance characteristic which is applied to a component, a single structure, or a structure consisting of different components. Structural integrity is the quality of an item to hold together under a load, including its own weight, resisting breakage or bending. It assures that the construction will perform its designed function, during reasonable use, for as long as the designed life of the structure. Items are constructed with structural integrity to ensure that catastrophic failure does not occur, which can result in injuries, severe damage, death, or monetary losses."

The structural integrity of your life and form is just as important as the structural integrity of a building. What you say and do has an impact on how you live. A lifetime of good things can come crumbling down in a moment with one wrong decision. For example, one bad choice to take drugs or drink too much alcohol can lead to a premature death. One wrong action of premarital sex can lead to a lifetime of STDs, HIV, or unintended pregnancy. One lie can collapse a friendship. One slander can destroy how people view you.

Maybe you've seen an adult in the news or in your own personal life who lost his job, his home, or even more because of a breach in his personal structural integrity. And remember when a building falls down, it doesn't just affect that building. It affects everything around it as well, leaving a mess in the air and on the ground.

For you to take your life further and advance through the different levels of life, your form must be intact. Your legs need to be strong with honesty. Your arms powerful with right choices (decency). Your body, mind, and spirit complete with sincerity and consistency in seeking and doing what is right.

It takes only a second for a person to lose a friendship or a future by a breach in integrity, just like it takes only a second for an entire building to fall.

Tony Evans

UP TO YOU

Circle the letter that best describes your response to the following statements.

1. If I had a friend who could get me into the theater to see a movie through a side door so that I didn't have to pay, I would do it.
   - **A** Definitely
   - **B** Maybe
   - **C** No, I wouldn't do that

2. If I knew that my parent(s) wouldn't approve of something, I would lie or not tell them about it so that I could do it anyway.
   - **A** Definitely
   - **B** Maybe
   - **C** No, I wouldn't do that

3. I go to websites where I can download videos and music without paying for them.
   - **A** Definitely
   - **B** Maybe
   - **C** No, I wouldn't do that

4. It is perfectly OK to copy homework as long as the other person doesn't mind.
   - **A** Definitely
   - **B** Maybe
   - **C** No, I wouldn't do that

5. I think about how my decisions and actions affect my family and/or friends.
   - **A** Definitely
   - **B** Maybe
   - **C** No, I don't do that

6. I think about how my decisions and actions affect people I don't know.
   - **A** Definitely
   - **B** Maybe
   - **C** No, I don't do that

7. It might be OK to break the law for an important cause.
   - **A** Definitely
   - **B** Maybe
   - **C** No, it would never be okay to break the law

8. Everyone who knows me would say they can count on me to be truthful.
   - **A** All of the time
   - **B** Most of the time
   - **C** Sometimes
   - **D** Never

9. I say and do things so that other people will like me.
   - **A** All of the time
   - **B** Most of the time
   - **C** Sometimes
   - **D** Never

INTEGRITY SCORE CARD			POINT TOTAL					POINT TOTAL
1.	A-2	B-4	C-6		6.	A-6	B-4	C-2	
2.	A-2	B-4	C-6		7.	A-2	B-4	C-6	
3.	A-2	B-4	C-6		8.	A-2	B-4	C-6	D-8	
4.	A-2	B-4	C-6		9.	no score recorded for this ?	
5.	A-6	B-4	C-2						

TOTAL POINTS

If your score was:

33-50: If you answered truthfully, you are walking in a high degree of integrity. You are doing the right thing, even when the right thing is difficult to do or might be unpopular. You are putting the welfare of others ahead of your own needs or wants.

28-32: If you answered in this range, take a moment to thank the people in your life who have taught you that it is important to do the right thing. You sometimes struggle with integrity when making decisions. Understand that acting out of conviction—what you know to be right and true—will become a habit if you are consistent.

16-27: Sometimes, we have to be awakened to the idea that the world is full of people, some of whom we may never meet, who count on us to do the right thing. Every time we get in a car to go somewhere, we are counting on everyone else to obey the traffic laws so that we can arrive at our destination safely. If your score is in this range, get into the habit of using the STAR principle as you make decisions.

The STAR principle tells us to Stop what we are doing, to Think about how our decisions will impact ourselves and others, to Adjust our decisions, and to Respond thoughtfully rather than to react emotionally.

Why we didn't score number 9

Number 9 is all about moral reasoning.

Do we think it was an act of integrity for Rosa Parks to refuse to give up her seat on the bus? It was against the law at the time. It also was against the law to hide Jews to save them from torture and death in Nazi death camps. The Pharisees said it was unlawful for Jesus to heal on the Sabbath. Question 9 looks at the motivations of the heart toward the well-being of others and whether the law in question is immoral or unjust. It is not a simple question.

No one likes finishing last. Meghan Vogel had already felt the rush of victory after winning her 1600-meter race. Just one short hour later she was lining up for a daunting 3200-meter. This second race couldn't have gone more differently than her first. On the final lap, not only was Meghan far behind her competition, she was on track to finish dead last: something she'd never experienced in a race.

That's when Meghan saw the only other girl left in the race collapse in front of her. Meghan didn't miss a beat, she caught up to the girl and helped steer her the rest of the way. Once they arrived at the finish line, Meghan fell back and made sure her opponent crossed the line ahead of her where she would have finished had exhaustion not set in.

While she was applauded for her sportsmanship, Meghan displayed an even more important virtue: integrity. The dictionary tells us that integrity is the quality of being honest and fair. While honesty and fairness are always worthwhile, they're rarely easy. These qualities become remarkable when no one expects them of you.

> ## Meghan saw the only other girl left in the race collapse in front of her.

Life has a way of being unfair, even when no one is at fault. Meghan saw something that seemed unfair happening to a competitor and took it upon herself to intervene. We all will face opportunities to benefit from other's loss. In those moments, instead of seeing an opportunity to add glory to your own name or giving into temptation to take the path of least resistance, think about how your actions can best bring glory to God. When you face your life with that kind of perspective, even failures can open to doors to spiritual successes.

You can read more about this story online by visiting us here:

go.tonyevans.org/athletes

In every sport there are boundaries and rules in place to maintain a sense of order within the game. Within these set boundaries and rules, a player or team is free to express themselves to the best of their ability on the field of play. But once a boundary is crossed or a rule is broken, the game must stop and a penalty must be enforced. When this happens, it is normally frustrating for the team or player that is penalized. However, the boundaries and rules are not to make the game frustrating for the players, but rather to maintain the integrity of the game that they play. To put it another way, without boundaries you would not have organized sports at all. Instead, you would be left with athletic chaos. The integrity of sports is dependent upon rules, and the execution of the rules contribute to the integrity of the game.

Integrity can be defined as the ability to maximize your potential while holding true to the rules and boundaries that have been set within the game. In order for true success to be obtained in life, there must be ethical, moral, legal, and—most importantly—biblical boundaries in place. These boundaries are not to constrict freedom, but rather to give you an environment where you can flourish without being penalized. In today's world, most people define freedom as a life with no boundaries. However, that is not a definition of freedom but rather a definition of chaos. How can someone be free to express themself as a player in life if their life is full of chaos due to a lack of integrity? You can be extremely talented, but if you lack the ability to showcase your skill within the boundaries, your gifts and talents will always be hindered. Therefore, success in life is dependent upon integrity and integrity will always contribute to true success.

Thirty years ago, states began to repeal the "Blue Laws" that prevented stores from being open on both Saturday and Sunday. While some business owners gladly opened their doors seven days a week in the hope of increasing sales, others gave themselves and their employees a day of rest, no matter what the law allowed.

One such businessman is Truett Cathy, founder of Chick-fil-A, now the second largest fast-food chain in the country. Sunday is a big day for fast-food restaurants, and a strong work ethic is no problem for Cathy, who opened a business at the age of 8 to help support his struggling family. But integrity can be seen throughout Cathy's business model: It doesn't matter where you are, if you walk into a Chick-fil-A, you will get the same high quality of food and friendly service every time. As far as a sandwich goes, a Chick-fil-A sandwich is one of integrity. Could Chick-fil-A add to the corporate bottom line by opening on Sunday? Very likely, the answer is yes. But the company has taken a position of integrity regarding taking a day of rest.

What about you?

As a Chick-fil A store operator, you could conceivably increase your income by over $100,000 per month and make a lot of hungry people happy by opening on Sunday. Cathy, a savvy and gifted businessman, knew that. His conviction about the Sabbath was more important to him than potential profits.

Is there something that you believe in strongly enough—have such a conviction about—that it would be worth giving up more than $1 million in income each year? Write it out: _____

_____

_____

How would the internal reward—the peace that comes from knowing you were true to what you believe—compare to the potential for having more money but less time to rest? _____

_____

_____

Define integrity in your own words. Explain why having integrity is very important in your life.

Evaluate your life experiences. Think of 2 times in which you were being dishonest. Explain why you were being dishonest? What were 2 lessons learned from your experiences? How can you apply it to your life?

Q & A

In assessing your dishonest acts, explain the process of regaining the trust back?

List 5 benefits of always telling the truth.

Visit go.tonyevans.org/athletes to view a clip from
the movie *Woodlawn* that will help you with your **form.**

KINGDOM KEY 3

WISDOM

1. You will distinguish between God's wisdom and the world's sayings.

2. You will explore negative consequences of bad choices.

3. You will understand where to find wisdom and how to get it.

WORD SKE

Reasonable
being in accordance with sound judgment and good thinking, making sense

Discernment
the quality of being able to grasp and comprehend what is obscure, art of perceiving

Apply
to put to use, especially for some practical purpose

Good sense of judgment, discernment—the abi.
to do more than understand, but also apply
understanding to life's decisions.

Origin of WISDOM: Middle English, from Old
English wīsdōm, from wīs wise. First Known Use
before 12th century

RULE BOOK

Real wisdom, God's wisdom, begins with a holy life and is characterized by getting along with others. It is gentle and reasonable, overflowing with mercy and blessings, not hot one day and cold the next, not two-faced. You can develop a healthy, robust community that lives right with God and enjoy its results only if you do the hard work of getting along with each other, treating each other with dignity and honor.

James 3:17

But if any of you lacks wisdom, let him ask of God, who gives to all generously and without reproach, and it will be given to him. **James 1:5** (NASB)

TRANSCRIBE
WRITE IN YOUR OWN WORDS

TRANSLATE
WHAT DOES IT MEAN?

HERE TO HELP with Tony Evans

Life is full of decisions, and I imagine that you might be like everyone else—tired of making the wrong ones. Some of us are still feeling the effects of the poor choices we made last year or the year before. If you were given some special coins you could cash in for a chance to leap backward through a few levels and redo the last few years, in light of what you know now, what would you do differently? Would you make better choices? Would you choose different friends? Or how about your time? Would you pick different ways of spending it? Would you have practiced harder at whatever sport, gift, or skill you have? Do your homework? (Okay, too far.)

If you answered yes to any of those questions, then you know what it means to apply wisdom to life's situations. Because that's exactly what you want to do. By answering yes, you want to go back and make a different choice, this time with the wisdom of hindsight.

Wisdom is the ability to not only understand the best way to approach something or someone, but also to do it. Wisdom might be a noun in English class but when it comes to living your life, it's a verb, an action. (Don't tell your English teacher that I said that.) But wisdom doesn't do you a bit of good stuck in your brain. You access the power of wisdom to get you to the next level only by applying it. By making choices in light of it.

Have you ever played a video game and made a bad choice? Maybe you went left when you should have gone right? Or you jumped when you should have run? Or you faced the evil "boss" when you didn't yet have the skills to defeat him? Oftentimes when that happens in a video game, your character, car, contraption, or whatever it is you are controlling zaps—poofs—disappears. You definitely don't get to move forward. In fact, sometimes you end up having to start all over way back at the beginning.

In life (thankfully) we don't get zapped—or poof—or disappear when we make unwise choices, or I don't think there would be anyone left on earth but Jesus. But our bad choices do set us back in other ways. They could:

Derail a friendship

Cause you to have to retake a class

Mess up your lungs or health

Ruin your reputation

Get you offtrack for college

Involve you in a car accident

Bring on discipline with your parents or school

Whatever it is, unwise choices end up stopping you from moving forward.

Wisdom, on the other hand, is a powerful key to unlocking doors to a better future, more enjoyable friendships, a possible romance, a greater position on the team or squad, a scholarship, testing out of college-level classes once you get there, the ability to afford a car, peace of mind when it comes to your physical body, and greater access to the power of prayer.

Wisdom moves you forward. Use this key to open doors, jump higher, run faster, defeat the enemy's schemes, and more!

Tony Evans

Circle the letter that best describes you. Then, follow the instructions to fill in your wisdom meter.

1. When I am not sure what to do, I look in God's Word for guidance.

Ⓐ Yes   Ⓑ No   Ⓒ Sometimes

2. When I am not sure of the best course of action, I pray about what to do.

Ⓐ Yes   Ⓑ No   Ⓒ Sometimes

3. I tend to repeat the same mistakes.

Ⓐ Yes   Ⓑ No   Ⓒ Sometimes

4. When I am faced with a tough decision, I seek counsel from others who have more experience than I do.

Ⓐ Yes   Ⓑ No   Ⓒ Sometimes

5. I don't talk to elderly people because they don't understand what my life is like.

Ⓐ Yes   Ⓑ No   Ⓒ Sometimes

6. I have at least one adult in my life that I can trust to give me good advice.

Ⓐ Yes   Ⓑ No

7. Friends my age are a good source of advice because they know what I am going through.

Ⓐ Yes   Ⓑ No   Ⓒ Sometimes

8. I base the advice I give others on how I feel about the matter.

Ⓐ Yes–they   Ⓑ No, I tell them   Ⓒ Sometimes
  asked me   to talk to a parent,
                       couselor, or mentor

9. I wait until I feel peaceful or calm, until I feel pretty sure about something, before I act or speak.

Ⓐ Yes, usually   Ⓑ No, I react   Ⓒ Sometimes I do
                          emotionally

10. I can remember a time when I followed advice that I didn't like, but I knew it was right.

Ⓐ Yes, and it   Ⓑ No, but I wish I had
  worked well   and I will next time.
  for me

WISDOM SCORE CARD

1. A. Fill the well up to the bottom hash mark   B. Fill the well half full   C. Fill the well only

2.	A	C	B	Answer:	

For the rest of the questions, fill in according to your answer:

3.	B	C	A	Answer:	

4.	A	C	B	Answer:	

Up to the next mark

5.	B	A	C	Answer:	

6.	A		B	Answer:	

Halfway to the next mark

7.	C	A	B	Answer:	

8.	B	C	A	Answer:	

Sorry, no ink

9.	A	C	B	Answer:	

10.	A	B		Answer:	

High school athletics are incredibly rewarding for the students who participate, but they're also highly stressful at times. Apollos Hester and his teammates from East View High School felt that stress firsthand in their game against Vandergrift. East View ultimately came out the winners of the tight football game, but only by a single point. Apollos was invited on air by a local news station for a post-game interview. That interview now has over 8 million views on YouTube.

Few people had heard such an inspiring and gracious message even from anyone, much less a high school football player. His words revealed a wisdom far beyond his age. Here's one of the most memorable quotes from that interview: *"It's an awesome feeling when you truly believe that you're going to be successful...regardless of the scoreboard...because you put in all the time, all the effort, all the hard work and you know it's going to pay off. And if it doesn't pay off, you continue to give God the glory...win or lose we realized, we were going to be alright...we're gonna keep smiling."*

Apollos surely hadn't won every game he'd ever played. He used wisdom he learned from past games, from his coach, and from God to shape his future attitudes and effort. Experience had taught him to never give up, to keep smiling, and that regardless of the final score everything was going to be alright. Then he took the platform of his team's success and used it to give God the glory. What resulted was the world being amazed at such wisdom coming from a teenager.

Apollos' story shows that, when you start applying yesterday's wisdom to today's actions, you'll find you are never too young, too small, too weak, too anything to be used for great things.

You can read more about this story online by visiting us here:

go.tonyevans.org/athletes

At the beginning of NFL training camp you receive a very thick playbook that is to be studied and understood throughout camp. It is extremely important to gain the knowledge and understanding of all of the X's and O's within the book. In order to have a shot at making an NFL team, it is essential that you know what to do when the ball is snapped. However, even though understanding the playbook is necessary to give you a chance of success in an NFL training camp, it pales in comparison to the importance of your ability to execute what you know. The NFL, just like any other sport, is a game of execution, not simply a game of information. You can study until you're blue in the face, but if you're unable to execute what you've studied, when there's opposition on the other side of the ball, you may be real smart, but you don't have a chance to see your name on the final roster.

While knowledge and understanding are very important, they are useless without wisdom. Wisdom is one's ability to take knowledge and understanding and put them to work within life's circumstances and obstacles. You may have memorized the Bible, but if you're unable to put its words into practice in your daily life, then you may be smart, but at the same time you are useless to your heavenly Coach. **To put it another way, knowledge will give you a chance but wisdom will give you a roster spot.** A successful life is not simply about knowing what to do. A successful life is intrinsically tied to doing what you know.

What is the difference between being smart and being wise?

What are things you can do to grow in wisdom?

Can you name one person you consider to be wise and explain why you chose them?

Does doing good things make you better than others? Why or why not?

THE ——
PLAYBOOK
LEVEL II
MY POWER

KINGDOM KEY 4

PRAYER

You will learn to develop a prayer list, jar, or journal.

You will discover a prayer pattern for praying through God's Word.

You will practice praying with someone else.

WORD SKETCH:

Abide
linger with, be around someone enough to know them well

Ask
to make a request of

Access
permission or the right to make use of something

Communication with and/or a petition to God.

Origin of PRAYER: Middle English, Anglo-French *priere*

First Known Use: 14th century

RULE BOOK

The prayer of a person living right with God is something powerful to be reckoned with. Elijah, for instance, human just like us, prayed hard that it wouldn't rain, and it didn't—not a drop for three-and-a-half years. Then he prayed that it would rain, and it did. The showers came and everything started growing again.

James 5:16

___TRANSCRIBE
WRITE IN YOUR OWN WORDS

TRANSLATE___
WHAT DOES IT MEAN?

Prayer is earthly permission for heavenly interference. **To put prayer last is to put God las**' **It is a kingdom teen's primary weapon of warfa**' **With it, you can touch heaven and change earth** The secret to prayer **is not in how long you pray or what kind of fancy words you pray;** it is in discovering God's will and then asking for it.

JUST FOR FUN

1. Create a prayer jar. At the beginning of each day, write a simple prayer on a rock or piece of paper and place it in your jar after offering up this prayer to God. You can place a prayer in the jar as many times as you would like throughout the week. The prayers can be whatever you feel like telling God. Share your prayers with your guide if you want. At the end of the week remove the pieces of paper from your prayer jar together and see how the Lord has heard your prayers and responded. Spend time remembering what God has done for you and thank Him for what He is going to do for you and through you.

(If you don't want to create a prayer jar, create a prayer list or a journal where you can add your prayers and then make a note when and how they have been answered.)

2. Spend time praying for very specific things with your group and/or guide: Grab a globe, spin it, and stop. Wherever your right pointer finger lands, pray for that country (the people, the government, the health care, the wars, the civil unrest, the economy, etc.); take a walk around your school or home and be specific in prayer over the places where you walk; pray for your future (your spouse, your children, your future job, your future place of residence, etc.).

HERE TO HELP with Tony Evans

Have you ever seen your parents or someone get a key in the mail attached to a letter or on the outside of an envelope? Sometimes car dealerships will mail out thousands of keys to thousands of people in order to try and lure them into their dealership. What they say in the letter is if you drive up to their dealership, sit in the prize car, put your key in and turn the ignition, and it starts, you win! Your key has just gotten you a brand new car!

If it doesn't start, your key isn't even worth the price of the postage it took to mail it to you. You might as well just throw it away.

Prayer is like a key. When it is the right key in the right car, amazing things can happen. After all, you are praying to the God who made and owns everything. But too many people don't know how to use this key. They don't feel like prayer "works" for them, so they throw it away. Maybe they stuck it in the wrong car. Or they tried to open a door with it or a locker at school. And since nothing happened, they assumed it was like one of those keys at the car dealership that wasn't worth much anyhow.

But God has given us the secret to the power of prayer. And He's made it plain. The secret to having this key working is Jesus Christ. He is the ignition that this key must fit in for it to work. Listen to what He says:

VERSE: **If you make yourselves at home with me and my words are at home in you, you can be sure that whatever you ask will be listened to and acted upon.** John 15:7

And in case you didn't understand what He meant in that verse, read this one:

VERSE: **From now on, whatever you request along the lines of who I am and what I am doing, I'll do it. That's how the Father will be seen for who he is in the Son. I mean it. Whatever you request in this way, I'll do.** John 14:13

He means it. Whatever you ask for along the lines of who Jesus is and what He is doing, He'll do it. So the secret of accessing the power of this kingdom key is not in the number of minutes you spend praying each day. It's not if you pray with your eyes open or shut. It's not even in how many times you toss in spiritual-sounding words like "Father, in heaven," or "Oh, great God." The secret to accessing the power of prayer is in hanging out (abiding) with Jesus, letting what He says hang out in your heart, and asking for things He wants you to do, have, be, and become.

The secret is in where you put this kingdom key. Put it in the ignition of Jesus Christ and what He's doing, where He's going, and what He wants you to do...and you win. He will open the door (Matthew 7:7). He will send the rain (Elijah). He will part the sea (Moses).

He will show you your way.

Tony Evans

1. **Pray Scripture.** Pick up a Bible and start reading. Select a verse such as, *"Truly, I say to you, as you did it to one of the least of these, my brethren, you did it to me"* (Matthew 25:45) and turn it into a prayer: *"God help me to reach out to the least of these in my world and to treat them as your loved children."* Or select a psalm as an inspiration for prayer. Try taking the Lord's Prayer (Matthew 6:9-13) and write your own translation in a way that reflects where you are in life.

2. **Give Thanks:** Using paper or a journal, make a word cloud or list of all the things in your life or in the world for which you are thankful. If you are feeling artistic, doodle images of all the things you are thankful for today.

3. **Discussion:** When you order something from the internet and are waiting for it to come, are you worried it's not going to arrive? Do you go back and order it again? And again? Or if you are at a fast-food restaurant and give them your order, do you keep telling them over and over while you wait? No, when you order it, you wait for it to come. This is because you are trusting and expecting it to come. The secret to living a life with the power of prayer is in knowing what to ask. Jesus says that if you ask anything that is in line with God's will, He will do it. Anything! List some things that you know are in line with God's will. I've given you a few to start with:

   A. Asking God to give you wisdom

   B. Asking God to reveal His purposes to you for your life

   C.

   D.

   E.

   F.

If you're a Monday night football fan you may be familiar with the tradition of the post-game prayer. The tradition began in 1990 after an especially tense game between the San Francisco 49ers and New York Giants. The teams' chaplains knew that, as the season's biggest Monday night game, there would be a lot of media attention, and they wanted to come up with a way to celebrate God. The idea of a joint prayer was their elegantly simple solution: Christians from both the winning and losing team would unite in their faith and give thanks.

The game itself lived up to all the hype. It was a close and tense match. As planned, after the clock ran out in the fourth quarter, a large group of players began to form at the 50 yard line, but it soon became clear that this was no prayer group. A fight had broken out between the teams. Slowly but surely, a small group of Christian players formed their own small huddle away from the brawl and took a knee together. The frenzy of the fight distracted most of the press and the prayer didn't get the coverage the chaplains had hoped. But, this small uncelebrated act began a now decades long tradition.

I love that the chaplains planned a group prayer after the game. It's easy to forget prayer is a two way street. It's not just a way to ask for what you want; it's also a time to listen to what God has to say to you. A lot of people forget that step, and then wonder why they're prayers aren't working for them. The players weren't praying to win or to be the MVP: remember the game was over. They were giving thanks and reflecting.

Whether you're on or off the field, maintaining your relationship with Jesus through prayer helps you discover your best self. Just like a team debriefs after a game, you should find time throughout the day to debrief with God. Win or lose, slow down and take a moment to give thanks and listen for the lessons God was showing you.

You can read more about this story online by visiting us here:

go.tonyevans.org/athletes

In a football game, when it's time for the quarterback to call a play, he will be listening to hear from the offensive coordinator through the speaker system that is integrated into his helmet. Throughout the entire game he will get instructions from this coordinator who is normally not on the field with him but rather in the press box high above him. The coordinator has the ability to see things that the quarterback can't see due to his location. He is looking down and seeing the big picture rather than the bits and pieces that the quarterback sees during each play. Whenever the quarterback has a question about what's happening on the field, he will just pick up the telephone on the sideline and call up to the coordinator. He does this because he knows that the coordinator has a greater perspective from higher up there than the quarterback does on the field. This communication with the coordinator gives the quarterback more firepower as he executes down low.

Prayer gives everyone the ability to communicate with God Who sits up high. God has a perspective that is much greater than any perspective of those on the field of play. He is looking down and seeing the big picture rather than the bits and pieces that man sees on the field. In order to see what He sees, we must be willing to pick up the phone of prayer and communicate with the heavenly Coordinator. The power of prayer contributes to the power of execution; it also contributes to a powerful holistic perspective. If there's a question about what's happening on the field, pick up the phone of prayer and let the Coordinator tell you what He sees. Unlike the offensive coordinator in a football game, the heavenly Coordinator is a perfect play caller who wants to call the plays in your spiritual headset. However, this Coordinator will not call the plays in your life until you pick up the phone.

What are some things that stop you from praying?

Can you describe a time that you prayed for something and God answered you?

Q & A

Do you think that God always answers our prayers? Why or why not?

What is the benefit of praying scriptures?

KINGDOM KEY 5

GOD'S WORD

1. You'll learn a formula (REAP) for understanding God's Word.

2. You'll practice reading God's Word and interpreting it to apply to your own life.

3. You will memorize key scriptures.

WORD SKETCH

Inspired
having a divine cause or influence

Truth
fidelity to an original or to a standard, the real facts about something

Powerful
having a strong effect on someone or something

"Scripture"–the sacred writings found in the Old and New Testament, the books of the Bible

Origin of GOD'S WORD: Middle English, from the Late Latin *Scriptura*

First Known Use: 14th century

RULE BOOK

There's nothing like the written Word of God....Every part of Scripture is God-breathed and useful one way or another–showing us truth, exposing our rebellion, correcting our mistakes, training us to live God's way. Through the Word we are put together and shaped up for the tasks God has for us. **2 Timothy 3:16**

God means what He says. What He says goes. His powerful Word is sharp as a surgeon's scalpel, cutting through everything, whether doubt or defense, laying us open to listen and obey. Nothing and no one is impervious to God's Word. **Hebrews 4:12-13**

___TRANSCRIBE
WRITE IN YOUR OWN WORDS

TRANSLATE___
WHAT DOES IT MEAN?

JUST FOR FUN

1. "Land Mine" Game (played with a group)—This game demonstrates the importance of listening to God's voice, which is made evident to us through His written Word. Split the group into two teams. On each team choose one member to be blindfolded and led through the "minefield." The minefield represents daily life and the obstacles Satan tries to place in our way. (The minefield can consist of water obstacles, barriers, things to step over, etc.). As the blindfolded member walks through the minefield, members on their team will guide them with words on how to maneuver through the obstacles. It is important for the blindfolded member to listen carefully to their team so that they do not get tripped up in the obstacles. To increase the difficulty of this game, have members of the opposite team try to distract the blindfolded member or, if you are outside, have other members of the opposite team throw water balloons at the one walking through the minefield. This demonstrates how important it is for us to know God's voice and how to distinguish it among all of the other "voices" in our world.

2. Memorize this week's verse and share it with your guide and/or group next time you meet. Some tips to help memorize it are to write it on a note card or sticky note and put it places you will see, or text it to yourself several times a day.

HERE TO HELP with Tony Evans

The Bible is a big book. To many people, it is a boring book. It's filled with names, dates, and stories set in different countries and different cultures in a different era. How is that supposed to help you know how to respond to someone gossiping about a friend of yours during third-period algebra class? You don't have time to dig through the 66 books to find out what it says about gossip, or look for a good way to respond to maintain your friendship with the person doing it, but also stand up for the one who is being hurt by the negative words. So what do you do with this thing that adults, Sunday school teachers, your pastor, coach, parents say you're supposed to use to "light your path"?

Can I answer that question by asking you another one? How do you eat an elephant?

One bite at a time.

I spent 12 years in college, seminary, and getting my doctorate (no, I'm not a medical doctor; it's what they call a doctorate in theology). I learned about the Bible all that time but I still have questions and things yet to discover. So I'm not expecting you to digest the whole thing after P.E. in study hall. Instead, take the Bible bit by bit...or bite by bite (going back to the elephant) as you start putting God's truth and principles inside of you.

It's like feeding your body. You don't eat a week's worth of food on Monday morning. You have a snack here, a protein drink there, or a meal there. Same thing with the Bible. Take a chapter in Proverbs and read it that day. In fact, Proverbs is so convenient because there are 31 chapters—one for every day of the month. Just read a chapter for whatever day of the month it is and if you forget a day, pick it up the next day.

Or if you want to discover some of Jesus' secrets for how He changed the world and want you to impact it as well, I'd encourage you to start reading through the book of John. Then maybe go to Luke. You can also use the Internet to search things like "Bible verses on gossip" and websites will come up that will give you a quick look at what God says about the topic. You could even do it on your phone while you're sitting there with your friend so you can know how to respond right then. And if you want to go a bit deeper in your understanding of this powerful kingdom key—God's Word—here's another tip called REAP.

R.E.A.P is an acronym to help you understand and use God's Word as a key to bring power to your life as you move forward. Here is how it works:

1. First you Read a passage or verse.

2. Then you Examine what is in the passage or verse. What sticks out? What questions do you have? What are some observations you make about this passage? Examine also includes making interpretations about the passage. What was God intending to tell us through this?

3. Next you Apply His Word to your everyday life. How can you practice what you have learned? Set goals and an action plan for yourself and to help those around you. "A" can also stand for "Accountability"; hold yourself or have someone hold you accountable for what you learned through this passage.

4. Lastly, Pray and ask God to provide opportunities to walk faithfully in the lessons you have learned and to use the knowledge and understanding you have gained to strengthen your relationship with Him, with others, and to strengthen you.

Tony Evans

se the verses listed for you in the lessons of this strategy guide, or pick your own verses to study. s you read them, use the SPECK method to see how it applies to you. Answer any or all of the uestions below from the verse. You can write them on your notes in your smartphone, on your blet, or in this strategy guide.

S—Is there a sin for me to avoid?

P—Is there a promise for me to claim?

E—Is there an example for me to follow?

C—Is there a commandment for me to obey?

K—Is there knowledge I can gain?

S _____
P _____
E _____
C _____
K _____

S _____
P _____
E _____
C _____
K _____

S _____
P _____
E _____
C _____
K _____

BONUS

When I was playing college football at Baylor University there were several times during the game when the defense would shift their position before the ball was snapped. What the opposing team was attempting to do was confuse our offensive execution before the play even started. We were certain about the play we were going to run from the playbook when we broke the handle, but when the defense shifted or moved, it could certainly become a distraction to the execution. Fortunately, our playbook that we studied to prepare for the game had all of the offensive answers to the defensive shifts. Without a working knowledge of the playbook we would panic and be defeated, but because we understood how to respond, we were able to progress down the field.

Life as everyone has experienced has the ability to shift, change, and move unexpectedly. Unfortunately, these changes catch a lot of people off guard and they panic and become defeated by life's sudden changes. However, God has given us a playbook called the Bible that has all of the offensive answers to life's defensive shifts. Without a working knowledge of God's Word we can easily be dismayed and defeated, but if we will take God's Word seriously, we will see that this playbook gives us the ability to know how to respond and therefore continue to progress down the field.

Jonathan Evans

Tim Tebow made a name for himself in the college football world as the quarterback for the Florida Gators. He was, and still is, equally well known for publicly displaying his Christian faith both on and off the field.

One of Tebow's most famous displays of faith was his eye black paint. He painted scriptures on the strips below his eyes. For all of his 2009 season, he used Philippians 4:13, "I can do all things through Him who gives me strength." It's a verse that many athletes find personally meaningful and inspiring.

Two days before the Gators' BCS National Championship game, Tim says he felt God was telling him to change the verse to John 3:16. His coach and his teammates were nervous: The Philippians verse had served them well all season. While they were well-intentioned, his team had begun to see the scripture tradition as a superstitious good luck charm. But, Tim listened to what God was telling him, and when he took the field he had the new scripture written below his eyes.

The Gators won the championship that year, but something much bigger happened. In the 24 hour period after the game, John 3:16 was the most Googled term with over 92 million searches. Millions of people searched and found one of the Bible's most important messages, "For God so loved the world that he gave his only begotten son that whosoever believes in him will not perish but will have everlasting life."

You don't have to be a Heisman winner before you can use God's word. You don't have to know the whole Bible, and you don't have to reach 92 million people before you can make a difference. Through prayer and studying, God will show you your unique opportunities to share His Word with others.

You can read more about this story online by visiting us here:

go.tonyevans.org/athletes

In every sport there are rule books dictating how the sport is to be played. These rule books are the governing guidelines that make up the context of the entire game. In other words, without the rule book there is no game. The creation of the rule book and the creation of the sport go hand-in-hand. If there is no rule book, there cannot be an organized sport. Conversely, if there's an organized sport, there will always be a rule book that governs it. The rule books are so important to sports that each sport will even have officials to make sure that the rule book is implemented correctly. Every individual playing within an organized sport will be cautious about the rule book as they make their decisions on the playing field. There is not one individual in all of sports who wants to be penalized during the game. Therefore, all athletes in every sport make sure that they know the rule book and that they are obedient to its laws. Unlike team playbooks, rule books cannot be reconfigured or changed based on the situation during a game. In other words, the rule books do not conform to the situation; the situation in every sport must conform to the rule book.

Likewise, in life we have been given a rule book by which all decisions are to be made on the field of play. This book is a perfect book written by a perfect Author. This perfect book is called the Bible. The creation of life and the creation of this book go hand-in-hand. If life is ever played outside of this book, penalties will follow. This book is so important in the game of life that there are even preachers and churches on every street corner explaining its principles and guidelines on a weekly basis. However, somehow the governing guidelines of athletics are taken more seriously than the governing guidelines of life. Most athletes are not as cautious to make sure they know and follow the guidelines of the Bible as they know and follow the guidelines of their sport. However, in order to have a good life with as few penalties as possible, the unchanging rule book called the Bible must make up the entire context of the game of life.

Visit go.tonyevans.org/athletes to view a clip from
the movie *Woodlawn* that will help you with your power.

KINGDOM KEY 6

FAITH

OBJECTIVES:

1. You will practice putting your faith in someone else to catch you.

2. You will learn how to apply faith through a life example.

3. You will score your own faith-meter.

WORD SKETC

Belief
a state or habit of mind in which trust or confidence is placed in some person or thing

Credence
mental acceptance as true or real

Trust
assured reliance on the character, ability, strength, or truth of someone or something

Strong belief or trust in someone or something; belief in the existence of God; strong religious feelings or beliefs

Origin of FAITH: Middle English *feith*, from Anglo-French *feid*, *fei*, from Latin *fides*; akin to Latin *fidere* to trust

First Known Use: 13th century

RULE BOOK

Now faith is the assurance of things hoped for, the conviction of things not seen.
Hebrews 11:1 (NASB)

It's impossible to please God apart from faith. And why? Because anyone who wants to approach God must believe both that he exists and that he cares enough to respond to those who seek him.
Hebrews 11:6

... for we walk by faith, not by sight.
2 Corinthians 5:7 (NASB)

But the Master said, "You don't need more faith. There is no 'more' or 'less' in faith. If you have a bare kernel of faith, say the size of a poppy seed, you could say to this sycamore tree, 'Go jump in the lake,' and it would do it." **Luke 17:6**

___TRANSCRIBE___
WRITE IN YOUR OWN WORDS

___TRANSLATE___
WHAT DOES IT MEAN?

JUST FOR FUN

Faith believes that God is who He says He is and has done or will do what He says He has done or will do. If this is a one-on-one situation, stand with your back to your guide and hold your arms out like a cross. Have the other person stand behind you so that they will be able to catch you when you fall backward.

Have the other person say, "I will safely catch you if you fall backward."

You are to respond, "I believe that you will catch me."

The other person says, "Fall back in 3...2...1...GO!"

At this point, with your feet planted on the ground, you will lean back and allow the other person to catch you.

In a group situation, have one member of the group stand on a chair in the same fashion as above. The rest of the group will form two lines facing each other with their arms interlocked with the person directly across from them, almost like a basket weave. They will form the "catch."

Repeat the same words as detailed above.

The focus of this exercise is to demonstrate a belief in the words of the other person or the group that they will do what they say they will do (catch you when you fall). Just as you are to demonstrate your belief in this, so you should demonstrate that you believe in God by the way you live your life because His Word is true and can be trusted.

HERE TO HELP with Tony Evans

A few years ago an interesting event occurred in South Carolina. I was scheduled to speak at a crusade at Williams-Brice Stadium, the football stadium of the University of South Carolina. The weather report had predicted rain. In fact, it had said that there would be a storm.

More than twenty-five thousand people had already gathered in the stadium and were waiting for the crusade to begin, when we saw the storm clouds forming. So we, the leaders and organizers of the crusade, wanted to pray that God would hold back the rain.

We went downstairs into a small room, gathered together, and began to pray. Of course, w prayed things like, "Dear God, please hold back the rain," and "If it's Your will, God, coul You hold back that rain?"

Yet in the midst of all of us praying, a petite woman named Linda came forward. Perhaps sh had gotten frustrated with the prayers of the so-called professionals—the preachers and th leaders.

Whatever the case, Linda stood up and asked, "Do you mind if I pray?" What else could w say but "Go ahead"?

Linda prayed, "Lord, Your name is at stake. We told these people that if they would come ou tonight they would hear a word from God. We told them they would hear from You. Now, they come and You let it rain and You don't control the weather, then You will look bad. W told them that You wanted to say something to them, and if You don't keep back what You ca control—the weather—someone could say that Your name is no good."

And then she threw in a line that caused us all to look at each other out of the corners of ou eyes. "Therefore right now I ask in the name of the Lord Jesus Christ for the rain to stop for th sake of Your name!"

With that, we opened our eyes. Eyebrows went up. All we could say and think was "Whoo Did she really just pray that?"

Following the prayers, we all went up and sat on the platform. The sky had now becom entirely black behind us. A guy who had been assigned to communicate directly with th weather bureau said, "The showers are coming. They are heavy thunderstorms, and they a coming right at us."

is now 7:00 p.m., and the music is beginning. It is time to start the crusade when massive thunder and lightning surrounded us. People began to stir in their seats. Some even started to get up and open their umbrellas. Linda was on the stage with the rest of us. While umbrellas began to go up in the audience, along with several on the stage, Linda sat there confident. A quiet look of expectation covered her face.

Then something happened that I have seen only once in my entire life. The rain rushed toward the stadium like a wall of water. Yet when it hit the stadium, it split. Half of the rain went on one side of the stadium. The other half went on the other side. Then it literally met on the other side of the stadium. All the while, Linda sat there with a confident look on her face. The rest of us, the preachers and leaders, just looked at each other. We looked at the rain going around the stadium, then we looked at each other again. Then we looked at Linda who just stared straight ahead.

Now, this is not a story that someone told me. I was there. In fact, my family was there with me. Not only that, but twenty-five thousand people were there with me too. And all of us saw a miracle that night right in front of our eyes. I believe that God paid special attention to Linda's prayer because she had great faith.

She knew God's name. She understood that His name represented His character. And her prayer appealed to that which mattered most to Him. She knew how to speak God's language.

I believe Linda's prayer ushered in a miracle because she realized that God is passionate for His own reputation and she put her faith in Him. Her petite frame held power, simply because she was intimately connected with and invested in God's name. Because the rain moved around the stadium, the crowd was protected so they could hear the gospel and respond with open hearts, having just witnessed a weather phenomenon.

> **Faith is a powerful tool in the hands of a kingdom teen.**

Faith is a powerful tool in the hands of a kingdom teen. The only time you are to do nothing is when there is nothing to do. Walk by faith. Unless it has hit your feet, it is not faith. God's calling on your life is bigger than what you can see. But He responds when you move—when you walk by faith, not wish by faith. For kingdom teens, faith is a verb. It is not passive. It is stepping out on the promises of God.

Tony Evans

Jack Hoffman was only five years old when doctors diagnosed him with pediatric brain cancer. His first surgery didn't go as planned and he required a second, riskier operation. Jack's parents wanted to do something special for him before he went back to surgery. So, they contacted his favorite sports team, the University of Nebraska football team.

> ## Jack Hoffman was only five years old when doctors diagnosed him with pediatric brain cancer.

The team invited Jack to campus, and his favorite player, Rex Burkhead, gave him a personal tour. Jack gave Rex a red bracelet that said "Team Jack Pray." From that moment, the bracelet never left Rex's wrist. He still had it on two days before Jack's surgery when Nebraska was playing it's opening game against Ohio. They were down 20-6 at halftime. In the locker room, Rex looked down and saw the red bracelet. He told his teammates, "Jack's not giving up and we're not giving up." The team rallied and staged the biggest comeback in Nebraska football history and won the game with a final score of 34-27.

Two days later, Jack mounted an even bigger comeback when he came through his surgery. Months later, Jack had recovered enough to actually play with the Nebraska team. In the fourth quarter of the spring game, Jack took the field and ran a 69 yard touchdown.

Life has a way of throwing what seems like unbeatable challenges at you. But, God has promised us that He's bigger than any of our enemies. Jack and his family didn't know how the surgery would turn out, but they knew they were in God's hands and that was enough to help them take the first step. But God can't stage a comeback for you until you get in the game. When it looks like you're facing the impossible, God wants you to give it your best and then trust Him to take care of the rest.

You can read more about this story online by visiting us here:

go.tonyevans.org/athletes

Most professional athletes have trainers they have hired to keep them in shape and show them how to be their best. These trainers are qualified and paid to make sure that the athletes they're training maximize their gifts and talents in their particular sport. However, in order to help the athletes maximize their talents and gifts, the trainers may ask the athletes to do stuff that they don't want to do, stuff that's hard and that pushes the athlete to the maximum limit of fatigue. This process is not something that happens every now and then, but rather every single day. Therefore, every day that athlete must do what the trainer says in spite of how the athlete feels about it. He or she must trust the trainer even though his or her body is entirely fatigued. In other words, even though the athlete may not totally understand or feel like doing what the trainer says, he or she must have faith that their trainer is truly qualified to make them their best.

Much like the trainer's relationship to the athlete, God is totally qualified to make us our best. He wants to make sure that you reach your maximum potential with the gifts and talents He has given you for His kingdom purposes. God wants you to not only reach your destiny but to be fully prepared for it when you get there. However, in order to prepare you, He may ask you to do things that you may not feel like doing, things that you may not totally understand. This training technique is not something you will experience every now and then, but rather every single day. Therefore, every day your job is to do what God says, in spite of how you feel about it. Whether you understand or feel like doing what your heavenly Trainer says is not the main concern. The main concern is whether or not you have faith that God is truly qualified to train you. Becoming your best as a person takes total faith in God as your Trainer. In other words, having faith is not avoiding fatigue, but rather doing what the Trainer says no matter how fatigued you get.

For each question, circle the number by the answer that best reflects the way you think and feel.

1. I believe that God's Word is always true, all of the time, in all circumstances, for all people.
   Ⓐ Strongly agree   Ⓑ Agree   Ⓒ Disagree   Ⓓ Strongly disagree

2. I tend to get discouraged when I am waiting on God to answer a prayer.
   Ⓐ Strongly agree   Ⓑ Agree   Ⓒ Disagree   Ⓓ Strongly disagree

3. In my life, I have experienced making a decision or acting on faith and being rewarded for it.
   Ⓐ Yes, many times   Ⓑ Occasionally   Ⓒ Maybe once   Ⓓ No, not that I know of

4. In my life, I have experienced making a decision or acting on faith only to be disappointed.
   Ⓐ Yes, many times   Ⓑ Occasionally   Ⓒ Maybe once   Ⓓ No, I have never been disappointed when I have acted on faith

5. Fear holds me back from trying new things.
   Ⓐ Strongly agree   Ⓑ Agree   Ⓒ Disagree   Ⓓ Strongly disagree

6. I need to see it before I can believe it.
   Ⓐ Always   Ⓑ Most of the time   Ⓒ Sometimes   Ⓓ No–if I can imagine it, I can believe it.

7. I make decisions based on how I feel about the situation or the people involved.
   Ⓐ Strongly agree   Ⓑ Agree   Ⓒ Disagree   Ⓓ Strongly disagree

8. I pray regularly to call on God for His help and guidance.
   Ⓐ Yes, at least once a day   Ⓑ Yes, often   Ⓒ Yes, every Sunday at church   Ⓓ Yes, when I am really worri or in a bind

9. I believe that God always answers prayer.
   Ⓐ Strongly agree   Ⓑ Agree   Ⓒ Disagree   Ⓓ Strongly disagree

10. Sometimes, things get worse before they get better.
   Ⓐ Strongly agree   Ⓑ Agree   Ⓒ Disagree   Ⓓ Strongly disagree

#					POINT TOTAL	#					POINT TOTAL	TOTAL POINTS
1.	A-5	B-4	C-3	D-2		6.	A-2	B3	C-4	D-5		
2.	A-5	B-4	C-3	D-2		7.	A-5	B-4	C-3	D-2		
3.	A-5	B-4	C-3	D-2		8.	A-5	B-4	C-3	D-2		
4.	A-5	B-4	C-3	D-2		9.	A-2	B-3	C-4	D-5		
5.	A-2	B3	C-4	D-5		10.	A-2	B-3	C-4	D-5		

your score was:

0-50: You have already learned the excitement of living by faith. God always answers ayer, but He doesn't always answer on our timetable or give us the answer we were seeking. The nger we walk with God, the more we learn that He always has our best interests in mind. We also rn that He is always true to His Word.

0-39: Building your faith, like anything else worth doing, requires practice. That practice mes through prayer, worship, and studying God's Word. When we "hide His word in our hearts," otherwise when we believe His Word to be true for all people, in all circumstances and at all times, hanges our perspective on life. We begin to see that sometimes what we wanted really isn't the best us, and we learn to trust that He will provide for all of our needs according to His riches and glory Jesus Christ (Philippians 4:19).

0-29: One thing is for sure: There is no condemnation for those who are in Christ (Romans 1). God wants you to have faith because through faith, He can bless you, provide for you, guide u, and otherwise make your life full. Never let anyone tell you that life with God is dull. Nothing n be further from the truth! Living by faith is the most exciting way to live. God wants to bless you undantly and above what you can dream or imagine (Ephesians 3:20). Start talking to God today. e is listening. Read His Word, and sing Him a love song. He is waiting!

OVERTIME

The African impala, like so many animals unique to that continent, is impressive in its beauty, form, and abilities. It also is considered a tasty morsel by several African carnivores, such as the lion, cheetah, and tiger! Unique to the impala is its ability to leap as far as 30 feet (10 meters) in length and as high as 3 meters (10 feet) in height. Even so, the impala can easily be kept in a zoo enclosure with a fence only 3 feet (1 meter) high because it will not jump if it cannot see where its feet will land.

You have no doubt heard the expression "to take a leap of faith." God made the impala to leap, but it won't unless it can see where it is going. You are made in the image and likeness of God (Genesis 1:27), and just like the impala, He has given you unique and beautiful gifts and abilities. He also has a plan for you—and it isn't to be eaten by a lion! Can you trust God to provide a landing place for you when

Can you be "semi-faithful" to someone or something? Please explain.

Can you describe a time when you struggled with doubt?
What did you do to rebuild your faith?

Q & A

Besides God, name three things you know to be true even though you have never seen them.

Finish this: Sometimes I don't believe...

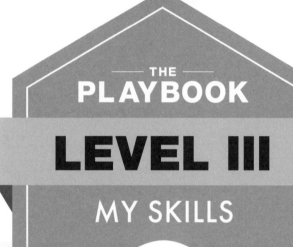

THE

PLAYBOOK

LEVEL III

MY SKILLS

KINGDOM KEY 7

RESPONSIBILITY

. You will learn how to prepare a budget and function on a cash system.

. You will make and keep a task chart.

. You will discover different areas in which you are to exercise responsibility.

Give
to transfer from oneself to another, either through time, talents, objects, or money

Reconcile
to restore a friendship, to make amends and reunite

Trusted
reality that someone or something is reliable, good, honest, effective, consistent, and dependable

able to be trusted to do what is right or to do the things that are expected or required

Origin of RESPONSIBILITY: Anglo-French *responsable*, from *respuns*. First Known Use: 1643

JLE BOOK

Responsibility in Relationships
his is how I want you to conduct yourself in these
natters. If you enter your place of worship and
are about to make an offering, then you suddenly
emember a grudge a friend has against you,
abandon your offering, leave immediately, go to
his friend and make things right. Then, and only
hen, come back and work things out with God.

Matthew 5:23

Responsibility in Helping Others
Whoever is generous to the poor lends to the Lord,
and he will repay him for his deed.

Proverbs 19:17 (ESV)

Responsibility to God
Honor God with everything you own; give him the
first and the best.   **Proverbs 3:9**

Responsibility in Leadership
The same goes for those who want to be servants
in the church: serious, not deceitful, not too free with
the bottle, not in it for what they can get out of it.
They must be reverent before the mystery of the faith,
not using their position to try to run things. Let them
prove themselves first. If they show they can do it,
take them on.   **1 Timothy 3:12**

RENDERING Responsibility concerns how you handle different areas of your life—whether that is your money, how you treat others, your time, your work, and any number of things. It could be as simple as taking your dishes back to the kitchen, rinsing them off, and putting them in the dishwasher, or as complex as showing integrity in your friendships or dating relationship. Responsibility means being trustworthy in any given situation.

JUST FOR FUN

Responsibility is being able to move with precision through your life to the determined goal or outcome without losing track of the details along the way. If responsibility is not a priority, that will be revealed when important things get lost, misplaced, are out of order or fall through the cracks while pursuing a particular goal.

The blind man's walk activity:
In this activity you will choose a partner. Within each partnership there will be one who guides and one who is led. However, the one who is led will be the one wearing a blindfold. The goal is to get from one side of the room to the other side of the room by following the directions of the guider without tripping over the obstacles along the way. There will be a special object on the other side of the room that the guider has to lead their partner across the room to retrieve. It is the responsibility of the blind folded partner to follow the directions of the guider precisely. It is the responsibility of the guider to give their blind partner precise directions. The team that handles their individual responsibilities the best and therefore retrieves the object first, wins the game!

On a team, others are dependent upon you taking care of your responsibilities. If one person is off the entire team will be negatively impacted.

HERE TO HELP with Tony Evans

our teens—right around your age—had been captured one day and
were taken to stand in the king's court. These four stood out among the
crowd. They were good looking, for starters. They were also easy to get
along with and always surrounded by friends. They were full of fun but
they also had the potential of a great future. They made great grades
and always got their school work turned in on time.

We know this from the verses where it says, "Then the king ordered
Ashphenaz, the chief of his officials, to bring in some of the sons of
Israel, including some of the royal family and of the nobles, youths in whom was no defect, who
were good-looking, showing intelligence in every branch of wisdom, endowed with understanding
and discerning knowledge, and who had ability for serving in the king's court. " Daniel 1:3-5 (NASB)

They were then enrolled in a three-year college of sorts—a king's college. The goal was to change
their thoughts from their ancestral culture and religion to that of the king's and his culture and religion.
They took classes and completed job responsibilities. Daniel and his friends were responsible in every
way. But they were also told to eat certain types of meat. So Daniel and his friends remained responsible in this area—responsible to keep their values in place.

The meat went against what Daniel and his friends' parents had taught them was clean, both for
their spirits and for their bodies. So even though they were young, they asked to be excluded from
those meals and given vegetables instead. They stood up to the king's orders and asked for special
consideration. Their parents didn't have to ask for them. Their parents didn't have to go to the school
officials to negotiate for them. After all, their parents were still back in their homeland. The men were
young, but they were on their own now. Their bold responsibility got them a hearing with the king's
council and they were given a test. The king decided to feed them what they requested for a period
of time and, after that time, to test how they looked and acted.

At the end of the test, the king and his council discovered that Daniel and his friends' "appearance
seemed better" (v. 15) and so they were allowed to continue. We also read that they found favor with
those who oversaw them and, over time, they even rose in leadership. In fact, Daniel eventually rose
to a position of great influence in the new land.

Responsibility means more than putting your dishes away after you are done eating, although that is
a good thing to do. It means more than getting your homework done and turning it in, also a good
thing to do. Responsibility means living a life in line with your values while also doing everything in
your power to meet the needs of those around you, including yourself. When you do these things, it
will not go unnoticed. And it will also enable you to reach your goals, to go further than you thought
possible, to gain the respect of others, and to make a difference anywhere and everywhere you are.

Tony Evans

1. Imagine you make $1,000 a month. Create a budget covering all required expenses. Discuss a▪ list some of those expenses with your guide and/or group.

MONTHLY BUDGET ($,1000)	
EXPENSES	**MONTHLY COST**
SAVINGS	
Savings Account	
BILLS	
Rent/Mortgage	
Utilities (Electric, Cell Phone, etc.)	
Groceries / Snacks	
CAR	
Car Payment	
Car Insurance	
Gasoline	
SHOPPING	
Clothes	
Other shopping	
FUN	
Entertainment	
Other Expenses	
EXPENSES SUBTOTAL	
NET ($1,000 minus Expenses)	

2. Understand what's going on with your spending by tracking your spending through a free servi▪ like mint.com. Review spending allotments and suggest changes.

Practice a 60-day cash-only envelope-based spending budget. This will help reinforce the value of money as you see where and how it is spent. For 60 days commit to use only cash, whenever possible. Write on envelopes the different areas you plan to spend such as: Food, Fun, Clothes, Tithe, Gas, etc. Based on your past spending habits and your budget, put the amount of cash in each envelope for each period of time until you receive cash again. When the envelope is empty, then refrain from spending in that area until you are able to fill it again.

Consider the different responsibilities you have depending on the environment you are in. Use the Responsibility Chart to list those and hold you accountable to them. This chart is a tool to help you stay on track with your responsibilities in each area. Write the name of the person who will keep you accountable at the top.

RESPONSIBILITY CHART

Week: _____

Accountability partner: _____

HOME	SCHOOL	COMMUNITY

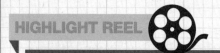

Athletes are responsible for a lot of things during a game, especially in team sports. They have to manage themselves as well as work fluidly with their teammates all while trying to stay one step ahead of the opposing team. That's not even mentioning nerves. Three middle school basketball players were in the middle of just that kind of pressure when they noticed something odd going on off court. Someone in the stand was making fun of one of their cheerleaders.

The cheerleader being picked on was eighth grader Desiree Andrews who has Down Syndrome. The three players stopped in the middle of the game and walked over to stand up for her and confront the bullies. To the boys, this kindness didn't feel like anything special. Desiree was their friend and they were simply taking responsibility for her well being. In fact, the team has even named their gym "D's House" in her honor.

Contrary to what many adults may think, teens have an incredible amount of responsibilities these days. Between balancing school, home, and social roles, stress levels can get high. When you already have so much on your shoulders, it can be easy to start looking at others' problems as just that: their problems. You can fall into the trap of telling yourself it's not your job to take on any more responsibility. But, God has told us that we are each others keepers.

It's ok and even necessary to think about yourself and your own needs, but we're also told to look out for the interests of those around us. The easiest place to start is with those close by. When you start to pay attention you may be surprised at how many opportunities, big and small, there are to show responsibility to those around you.

You can read more about this story online by visiting us here:

go.tonyevans.org/athletes

GAME ON with Jonathan Evans

Football is one of the most adrenaline pumping, emotionally arousing games on the planet! The players run out of the tunnel to the sound of 100,000 yelling fans, and listening to the national anthem with fighter jets flying over the stadium. Fireworks light up the skies and music rocks the stadium as the first kickoff approaches. There is no question that the emotions, anxiety, and adrenaline in the bodies of these players are off the charts. However, no matter how much emotion is conjured up for an NFL football game, emotions do not determine the outcome of the game. After the jets have flown by, the fireworks have dissipated, the music is over, and the players have taken the field, the attention for each player moves from physical emotion to practical responsibility. The question is, Can you do your job?, not, How do you feel about doing your job? A player's emotions will fluctuate through the course of the game depending on the situation. However, no matter what the situation, the responsibility to the playbook stays the same. The truth is, the player's emotions only determine his feelings, but a player's attention to his responsibility determines his outcomes.

Much like the beginning of a football game, you have several times in life where you are excited about where life is taking you. However, as the game of life continues and you experience different situations on the road to your purpose, you may find that your feelings of excitement tend to dissipate. Whether you are excited, disappointed, happy, sad, in love, angry, anxious, tired, or even afraid, the question will always be, Can you do your job? Are you willing to take care of your responsibilities consistently, even when your emotions are inconsistent? In other words, no matter what the situation, your responsibility to the playbook of life stays the same. Therefore, your emotions may be real but if they prevent you from executing your responsibilities to the playbook, they become real irrelevant. Emotions only determine your feelings, but your attention to your responsibilities will always determine your outcome.

What are some of the benefits of being responsible at home, in friendships, at school, etc.?

What are three areas that you can grow in responsibility? What steps can you take?

Does being responsible scare you? Why or why not?

Who is responsible for you?

KINGDOM KEY 8

SERVICE

OBJECTIVES:

1. You will discover different levels of service.

2. You will find ways to serve others.

3. You will be able to define what service means to you.

WORD SKETC

Assist
to give support or help; to make it easier for someone to do something or for something to happen

Help
to do something that makes it easier for someone to deal with something, to aid or assist someone

Esteem
the regard in which one is held; especially high regard

a *useful act meant to help someone els* or *a group of people*

Origin of SERVICE: Middle English, fron Anglo-French *servise*

First Known Use: 13th century

RULE BOOK

Be quick to give a meal to the hungry, a bed to the homeless—cheerfully. Be generous with the different things God gave you, passing them around so all get in on it: if words, let it be God's words; if help, let it be God's hearty help.
1 Peter 4:10

It is absolutely clear that God has called you to a free life. Just make sure that you don't use this freedom as an excuse to do whatever you want to do and destroy your freedom. Rather, use your freedom to serve one another in love; that's how freedom grows. **Galatians 5:13-14**

This is my command: Love one another the way I loved you. This is the very best way to love. Put your life on the line for your friends. **John 15:13**

___TRANSCRIBE
WRITE IN YOUR OWN WORDS

TRANSLATE___
WHAT DOES IT MEAN?

To demonstrate true humility by seeking, serving, and protecting the well-being of others.

JUST FOR FUN

1. In your own words, what does service mean to you?

2. Volunteer in a soup kitchen or food pantry with your guide and afterwards discuss how it made you feel to serve those who are less fortunate than yourself. Brainstorm ways in which you can offer up your life to serve those around you and discuss these with your guide or group.

3. Play "Secret Service." In this game, you are a Secret Service agent who secretly serves someone on your team in an ongoing basis for one month. At the end of the month, you can reveal your identity and hear their response to having been served.

Write down who you are going to serve: _____

List some ways you can serve that person. Ask your guide for ideas as well.

_____

_____

_____

HERE TO HELP with Tony Evans

Serving comes in a variety of forms. It could mean doing something for someone or even encouraging them with what you say. It rises out of a heart that esteems the other person as valuable and makes it easier for them to deal with whatever situation they are in. It might be as simple as picking up an extra lunch for a friend when you go through a drive-through and bringing it back, or as detailed as helping with some other teens to do a parking lot trash pick-up one Saturday morning, or going on a missions trip to help those who don't have clean water or enough food. It might even mean giving up your life so that others can live, as we'll see in this session's Life Link.

The same Jesus who came to give us life is the same Jesus that asks us to take up our cros and to do so daily. Service ought to be motivated by more than a desire to cross off a list; ought to be a way of life—a mindset.

In fact, God tells us the reason He created us was for service. We read in Ephesians, "For w are His workmanship, created in Christ Jesus for good works, which God prepared before hand so that we would walk in them" (2:10). You were created by God for "good works That's exactly what it says. So if you are ever standing around wondering why on earth yo are here, you have your answer right there: to do good. A "good work" involves an action c activity that benefits others while bringing glory to God. Essentially, it's serving.

Whether that service comes in a one-time action such as passing out additional Christma presents to needy families, or giving the mailman a bottle of water when he comes to you door in the summer, or whether it is a more long-term commitment to the betterment of anot er—all service matters to God.

And it's exactly why you are here. You are here to serve and to bring good to those aroun you. If that is your baby sister, parents, friends, teachers, or some people you don't knov who live halfway around the world whom you travel to on a missions trip, then doing "goo works" for God is a critical reason why you are here, and why you were created in the firs place. Service is not based on feelings. It's based on simply doing what you were put here t do. You shouldn't only serve when you feel like it.

Let me ask you a question: What would you do with a refrigerator that didn't feel like gettin cold, or a stove that didn't feel like getting hot, or a can opener that didn't feel like openin any cans? You would probably replace them with appliances that would work. You woul have to conclude that the refrigerator, stove, and can opener simply didn't understand th reason they had been chosen to be in your kitchen.

You have a role to play in this world. An important role. And when you play it well, peopl will know that you are a person who can be counted on to bring good wherever you go.

Keep in mind a careful distinction that needs to be made concerning service. Service that i done with a right heart attitude is service that is done expecting nothing in return. It is offere that God might be glorified and others benefited. Doing something for someone else an then expecting them to do something for you in return is called business, not service. An while there is nothing wrong with doing business, you just need to understand that it is onl service when it is done to glorify God and help someone else. No matter how small nor hov big the action, when accompanied by the right spirit of service, God takes notice. He ha created you for a life of greatness, and that greatness comes by walking the path of service

Tony Evans

each question, circle the answer that best describes your thoughts and attitudes regarding serving others.
n tally your score.

My family serves the community together.

Ⓐ Yes, we do that
regularly

Ⓑ Yes, we have done
that a few times

Ⓒ We did that once,
but it was hard work

Ⓓ No, we have
never done
anything like that

I have had an experience in my life when I served others and it made me feel:

Ⓐ Scared

Ⓑ Tired, dirty,
and hungry

Ⓒ A and B, but
it was also fun

Ⓓ Very fulfilled and
happy. I couldn't
wait to do it again.

If I see someone who could use help opening a door or something, I help without being asked.

Ⓐ Yes, frequently

Ⓑ Yes, especially if they
are elderly or disabled

Ⓒ I think about it,
but I am embarassed
to try

Ⓓ No, it's not my
business

Earning money for the things I want is at least partially my responsibility.

Ⓐ True, and I do

Ⓑ I think this is true
but I don't do it

Ⓒ I have not really
thought about this

Ⓓ No, that's what
parents and
relatives are for

An important way of expressing that I follow Christ is by serving others.

Ⓐ No, people should
help themselves

Ⓑ No, my relationship
with God is personal,
between me & Him

Ⓒ Maybe, but some
people serve and it
doesn't have any-
thing to do w/ faith

Ⓓ Yes. Helping
others is a way of
showing love &
compassion and
awakening those
things in my heart

When I serve, I expect nothing in return.

Ⓐ True. If you're
expecting something
back, that's not
service

Ⓑ True, but sometimes
people do give you
something, and that
makes them feel good

Ⓒ I know I shouldn't
expect anything,
but I am hopeful

Ⓓ One of the
important parts
of serving is that
you get rewards
& recogniztion

There are plenty of other people, and even the government, who can help the poor better than I can.

Ⓐ True. That's what
the government
and charities are for

Ⓑ True. There's not
much I can do to
make a difference

Ⓒ I could probably
help, but no one has
asked me to get
involved

Ⓓ True, but I can
make a big
difference in
someone else's life

When someone else serves me, I feel:

Ⓐ Humbled and
grateful; it makes
me want to give back

Ⓑ Humbled and
thankful, but I want
to crawl in a hole
and hide

Ⓒ Proud! It's about time
somebody saw the
need and helped

Ⓓ Embarassed and
a little angry. I
don't want to help

9. Someone in my church or school has approached me about getting involved in a service project.

Ⓐ Yes, I did it and I loved it!

Ⓑ Yes, and I did it because we have a community service requirement at school

Ⓒ I thought about it, but I decided not to do it

Ⓓ No one has eve approached m about serving

10. I have identified areas of need that I love to serve and people groups that I really enjoy helping.

Ⓐ True. I have a vision for serving more and bigger in the future

Ⓑ I love to serve, but I haven't yet identified a target that ignites my compassion

Ⓒ Not really. I serve because it is expected of me

Ⓓ No, I have not really done mu service

SERVICE SCORE CARD				POINT TOTAL						POINT TOTAL		TOTAL POINTS
1.	A-5	B-4	C-3	D-2		6.	A-5	B-4	C-3	D-2		
2.	A-2	B-3	C-4	D-5		7.	A-2	B3	C-4	D-5		
3.	A-5	B-4	C-3	D-2		8.	A-5	B-4	C-3	D-2		
4.	A-5	B-4	C-3	D-2		9.	A-5	B-4	C-3	D-2		
5.	A-2	B3	C-4	D-5		10.	A-5	B-4	C-3	D-2		

If your score was:

40-50: You have already benefited from plugging into service at your church or anoth service-oriented group and you are reaping the benefits that result in your soul—your mind, will, a emotions. Be sure to thank the adults in your life who have made these opportunities possible for yo You have experienced the true humility that results from knowing that God wants to and can wo through you to empower and enrich the lives of others. If the Lord has given you a vision for missio or serving others in a big way, pursue it with all that you are.

30-39: You have experienced the benefits of serving to a degree. Consider making servi a higher priority in your life. Are there activities you do that don't really produce much fruit in your lif If you are insensitive to the needs of others or find yourself turning away or avoiding situations wh you see others in need, pray and seek counsel about why your heart may be hard in those area There may be wounds that need healing, and Jesus can do that. Read the beatitudes (Matthew 5 12) to discover the blessings that Jesus has for you through service.

20-29: Since community service is a requirement in so many schools, and since colle admissions offices are looking for service on your resume, opportunities abound. God is calling y to get out of your comfort zone and plug in. Service is guaranteed to stir your soul in powerful way If your first experiences don't deliver on this guarantee, keep searching for an opportunity that w If your family is not serving, you can be the catalyst to ignite a powerful change in your home. Ta some time in prayer and reflection and ask the Lord to shift your mindset away from a consumer that of a giver.

In November of 2010, University High School's girls track team was set to become California's State Champions. It was a particularly emotional accomplishment as the team had dedicated their season to their coach, Jim Tracy. Tracy was suffering from amyotrophic lateral sclerosis, also known as Lou Gehrig's Disease.

With only a final 3.1 mile race left to complete, University High placed their hope in their top runner, 16 year old Holland Reynolds. Reynolds finished the first two miles without any problems, but at the final mile she began to slow. As the other runners began to zoom past her, she ultimately collapsed only yards from the finish line. An official came to offer assistance but explained that if she accepted help she was disqualified. Knowing that all she had to do was cross the finish line, Holland refused help and began to crawl. Over 20 seconds later, she crossed the line.

Holland's story is a remarkable example of the power of service to others. Although they didn't know it at the time, the team's state championship was already clinched. They didn't need her to finish that race, but her incredible effort became the most powerful testament of their love for their coach.

When we set our sights on goals bigger than our own glory, we start to discover a power we didn't know we had. Holland wasn't racing for herself. She was racing for her coach and against the cruel disease that had stolen his ability to run.

If you only measure success against self-serving victories, you'll inevitably end up disappointed. No one wins all the time, because we weren't created for that purpose. When you start to measure your success against what you have done for others, you'll be amazed at the kind of champion you can be.

You can read more about this story online by visiting us here:

go.tonyevans.org/athletes

Tennis is one of the few sports where you don't have to rely on a team to get the job done. Each individual player on the court can win the game based on their own decisions and athleticism as they ping the ball back and forth. However, there is one key component to the game of tennis that must be strong in every individual tennis player's game to experience success. This primary skill, if not utilized, will leave any player with a minimal chance to win. This skill and primary component is having the ability to serve. Serving in the game of tennis gives a unique opportunity for a player to place the ball exactly where they want it on the other side of the court. It also gives the player the unique opportunity to control the power and speed of the ball to the other side of the net. Any tennis player would admit that they would prefer to serve than to be served. Or to put it another way, they would rather be on the giving end than the receiving end. While there are many components that make up a successful tennis career, having a strong, powerful, accurate serve is the key.

There are many components that the world believes make up a successful individual. However, the picture that is drawn by the world of success does not include service. Actually, the picture of success in the world is quite the contrary. If you are being served that means you have reached a high level of success. If people are waiting on you hand and foot and doing everything that you say as the boss, then you are viewed as successful. While that picture of success may be true for the world, it is not true for the kingdom of God. I would think that Jesus Christ was successful in His life on earth, and the last time I checked, He said, "I have come to serve not to be served." In other words, a person who is looking to be great for God would prefer to serve, not simply be served. Or to put it another way, they would rather be on the giving end than the receiving end. Therefore, if your goal is to be great on the court of this world, then you will strive to be served, but if your goal is to be great in God's economy, you will look to do the serving. While there are many components that make an individual great in the kingdom of God, having the willingness, desire, and ability to serve others is the key.

In what ways do you enjoy being served?

Do you think that service and sacrifice is the same thing? Why or why not?

Is service a requirement?

Do you enjoy meeting the needs of other people?

In what ways have you served someone in your personal life?
(A friend, a stranger, a community, etc?)

Visit go.tonyevans.org/athletes to view a clip from
the movie *Woodlawn* that will help you with your **skills.**

KINGDOM KEY 9

SELF-CONTROL

OBJECTIVES:

1. You will learn what the Bible says about self-control.

2. You will see that athletes need self-control both on and off the field.

3. You will take a quiz to discover how self-controlled you are.

WORD SKETC

Willpower
the ability to control yourself; strong determination that allows you to do something difficult

Composure
a calmness or repose especially of mind, bearing, or appearance' self-possession

Restraint
control over your emotions or behavior

restraint exercised over one's own impulses, emotions, or desires

Origin unknown

First recorded use: 1711

ANCIENT TEXT

Put these verses in a simple code, such as each letter moved one ahead in the alphabet. (An a becomes a "b." A b becomes a "c," and so on. For example, person = qfstpo.) Text the coded verse to a friend and ask him/her to crack the code. Be sure to give a clue if your friend is stumped.

A person without self-control is like a house with its doors and windows knocked out.
                                                                         Proverbs 25:28

For God gave us a spirit not of fear but of power and love and self-control. Timothy 1:7 (ESV)

___TRANSCRIBE
WRITE IN YOUR OWN WORDS

TRANSLATE___
WHAT DOES IT MEAN?

HERE TO HELP with Tony Evans

In 1947, Jackie Robinson forever changed the landscape of not just baseball but also our country by becoming the first African-American "to compete in Major League Baseball in the modern era."* To give you some historical context, US racial desegregation was in its infancy. It would be seven years before the Supreme Court mandated that black and white students attend the same public schools. And it would be eight years before Rosa Parks made her now-famous bus ride that sparked Montgomery, Alabama, bus boycotts and gave a boost to the Civil Rights movement.

Jackie's indisputable talent and unselfish style helped him win the hearts of his teammates and colleagues. However, one of the most important values Jackie displayed during his time with the Dodgers was his self-control. Racism, not the opposing teams, was his greatest opponent. More than his unparalleled athletic skill and more than his team spirit, his self-control was his greatest asset.

While today it's well known that Jackie faced strong racism on and off the field, including death threats aimed at him and his family, he never took the bait to retaliate. To understand the magnitude of his self-control, you have to know more about the man Jackie was. Jackie was naturally inclined to stand up and push back against injustice. In fact, while serving in the army during WWII, he faced a general court-martial charge for refusing to move to the back of a military bus. Fortunately, he was exonerated by the court.

Because of his great courage, Jackie found it even more difficult to meet unjust hatred with silence. Holding back public retorts didn't come easily for Jackie. But the space formed by his silence was filled by undeniable talent and dignity that ultimately did more to muffle his detractors than his words could.

Life will challenge you. It will be tempting to react hastily or give in to your knee-jerk reactions. Sometimes, as in Jackie's case, those reactions may even be justified. But God uses challenges to help shape us into our best form. Exercising self-control can mean the difference between your being stuck where you are or leveling up to a stronger, better you.

Tony Evans

For each question, circle the number by the answer that best reflects the way you think and feel.

1. My typical behavior pattern is:

Ⓐ Feel-Act   Ⓑ Act-Think-Feel   Ⓒ Feel-Think-Act   Ⓓ Stop-Think-Act

2. I am often tempted by desires that are at odds with my values or beliefs.

Ⓐ Yes, regularly   Ⓑ Sometimes   Ⓒ Seldom   Ⓓ Rarely

3. People have told me that I am impulsive.

Ⓐ Yes, I frequently hear this   Ⓑ Sometimes   Ⓒ Seldom   Ⓓ Never–they tell me to be more spontaneous

4. I have set boundaries for myself that I simply do not cross.

Ⓐ Yes, that is true   Ⓑ I set them, but I do cross them sometimes   Ⓒ My boundaries are set by others   Ⓓ I don't believe in boundari

5. I resist it when those in authority over me set boundaries for me.

Ⓐ I don't like it, but I go along with it   Ⓑ Yes, most of the time   Ⓒ Yes, sometimes   Ⓓ No, I appreciate the boun

6. I find it easy to resist temptation.

Ⓐ Always   Ⓑ Most of the time   Ⓒ Seldom   Ⓓ Never

7. When I need self-control, I pray to God for help.

Ⓐ Yes, and it helps   Ⓑ Yes, if I remember to   Ⓒ Only when I think I may get in trouble   Ⓓ No

8. I sometimes think or act in ways that block my progress toward my goals.

Ⓐ Yes, almost always   Ⓑ Yes, sometimes   Ⓒ Yes, but I usually catch myself   Ⓓ Not really; I am able to ke on track

9. Other people can easily talk me in or out of doing things that I know are wrong.

Ⓐ Yes, this happens a lot   Ⓑ Often, but it depends on who the people are   Ⓒ Often, but it depends on what's in it for me or my friends   Ⓓ No, I think about how who I say will affect and influe others

10. When I have money in my pocket or purse, I spend it.

Ⓐ Yes! There's so much stuff I need   Ⓑ Yes. I try to save, but it's hard   Ⓒ No, I save up for what I really want   Ⓓ No, I never spend money

SELF-CONTROL SCORE CARD				POINT TOTAL					POINT TOTAL	TOTAL POINTS
1.	A-2	B-3	C-4	D-5		6.	A-5	B-5	C-3	D-2		
2.	A-2	B-3	C-4	D-5		7.	A-5	B-4	C-3	D-3		
3.	A-2	B-3	C-4	D-5		8.	A-2	B-3	C-4	D-5		
4.	A-5	B-4	C-3	D-2		9.	A-2	B-3	C-4	D-5		
5.	A-5	B-4	C-3	D-5		10.	A-2	B-4	C-5	D-2		

your score was:

3-50: You are walking in a high degree of self-control. Keep up the prayer and Bible study, keep thinking things through before you speak or act. Your rewards will come in due time.

5-42: You have self-control, but you are wavering and letting your willpower weaken at s. Remember that your will is a part of your soul, and it should be kept in line with your mind ugh prayer and the leading of the Holy Spirit.

7-34: You may find that you make impulsive decisions and lack self-control or that you uently are led by your emotions. Emotions are not bad, but you should examine them to find out root cause. Be sure you are considering your values and beliefs. Ask yourself what is important ou, and what you believe to be true. Self-control will enable you to channel your emotions structively.

0-26: Whoa! Your emotions and lack of self-control may be getting you in hot water at ool, at home, or in your relationships. Remember the STAR principle—Stop, Think, Act, and Respond way to exercise self-control. (See page 12 of the Kingdom Quest strategy guide.) A response is erent from a reaction. Self-control requires training. Keep practicing! It's worth it. Self-control is also it (evidence) of the Holy Spirit's presence in your life. So keep spending time with God so this fruit be more evident in your life.

RENDERING When faced with challenging situations, your ability to control your response and reaction is critical to long-term success. Self-control also involves recognizing and getting ahead of any problems or temptations through intentional action.

Olympic gymnasts are some of the greatest athletes in the world. These men and women have an incredible ability to jump, run, tumble, and—most of all—display the ultimate physical control in the world of athletics. During the Olympic Games, these gymnasts are not only judged on every facet of their athleticism but also on their form and self-control. The female gymnast's ability to do a back handspring on the balance beam is discounted if she doesn't display the control to stay on the beam when she lands. A male gymnast's athleticism on the rings is irrelevant if he doesn't display the strength and self-control to maintain balance. Gymnasts must display their talents while simultaneously maintaining total self-control. Athletic talent for a gymnast is vitally important; however, athletic talent without self-control will not produce a medal-winning Olympian.

The apostle Paul understood this concept. He wrote, "Every athlete exercises self-control in all things. They do it to receive a perishable wreath, but we an imperishable" (1 Corinthians 9:25, esv). God has given everyone gifts and talents to accomplish great things in life. But also keep in mind that everyone does not possess the same level of talent or the moral compass and self-control to maximize those gifts and talents. If everyone had the same measure of talent, then the question is this: What separates those who experience success in an area and those who do not? Self-control is part of the answer. While everyone has the talent to get on the beam of success, not everyone has the self-control to stay on it. While everyone has the talent to grab the rings of opportunity, not everyone has the strength and self-control to stay balanced. Having an opportunity for success will come with your natural talent, but to have the ability to sustain success in God's economy, a person's life must be under the control of the Holy Spirit.

You can read more about this story online by visiting us here:
go.tonyevans.org/athletes

GAME ON with Jonathan Evans

As athletes there are parts of our makeup that are natural to feel during the course of a competition. Every competitor has experienced the natural feelings of happiness, joy, anger, anxiety, anxiousness, and an array of other feelings that are conjured up due to competitive circumstances. Different scenarios will bring up different feelings naturally and there is nothing wrong with that; it is just the way things are. However, even though a game situation may prompt certain feelings, this doesn't always mean that it's appropriate to display what you feel. In other words, there are times when it's okay to display your natural feelings and there are times where acting on what you feel would be inappropriate or not be a benefit to the outcome of the game.

As human beings it is natural to feel a desire for the opposite sex. That desire is not only natural but also God-given for everyone in the game of life. However, just like in any competition, just because something is natural doesn't mean it doesn't require self-control. Sex is a great thing that is natural and created by God, but it has somehow become a big problem. In the United States, 800,000 teen girls get pregnant per year. One out of every four teens is infected with a sexually transmitted disease. The poverty level is continually increasing due to the dropout rate of young teen parents. Not to mention the emotional scarring that takes place due to the misuse of sex, which is unmeasurable. How could this much mess come from something so natural given by God? Simple. Just because something is natural doesn't mean it's always appropriate. God as the head coach has created sex for the game of life, but He has designed that play to only be run in the context of marriage.

Sex in marriage is like fire in a fireplace. When contained in its proper environment, it brings warmth and comfort. But when allowed to run free, it can bring destruction. Just as self-control is needed for victory on the field, it is needed even more for victory in life.

What is wrong with having too much of a good thing?

What is one thing in your life that you have too much of?

Q & A

At Home?

At School?

With Friends?

What is the opposite of self-control?

THE

PLAYBOOK

LEVEL IV

MY BRAND

KINGDOM KEY 7

COMMUNICATION

. You will learn the key components of good communication.

2. You will discover what is appropriate for social media.

3. You will discuss the distraction of cell phones in face-to-face communication.

Nonverbal
communicating without using words

Talk
to say words in order to express your thoughts, feelings, opinions, etc., to someone

Listen
to hear what someone has said and seek to understand it

WORD SKETCH:

the act or process of using words, sounds, signs, or behaviors to express or exchange information or to express your ideas, thoughts, feelings, etc., to someone else

Origin of COMMUNICATION: Latin *communicatus*, past participle of *communicare* to impart, participate

First Known Use: 1526

RULE BOOK

Watch the way you talk. Let nothing foul or dirty come out of your mouth. Say only what helps, each word a gift. **Ephesians 4:29**

They make a lot of sense, these wise (people); whenever they speak, their reputation increases. **Proverbs 16:23**

The right word at the right time is like a custom-made piece of jewelry. **Proverbs 25:11**

___TRANSCRIBE
WRITE IN YOUR OWN WORDS

TRANSLATE___
WHAT DOES IT MEAN?

JUST FOR FUN

1. Communication is key, but communication involves a whole lot more than just word And when communication does involve words, it is important to choose your word wisely and according to what is best for the situation you are in. In this activity, as group you will form a human knot. Have everyone stand in a circle and put his or h right hand in the middle of the circle. Instruct them to grab the right hand of someor who is not standing immediately adjacent to them. Once this is accomplished, hav them do the same thing with their left hands, adding that they cannot grab the left har of someone they are already grabbing the right hand of. You cannot speak during th activity. Afterwards, discuss as a group the importance of the words and actions we u: when we communicate. Also discuss ways in which communication goes wrong or cc be misunderstood, especially over social media or through text messages.

2. Brainstorm, with those you are with, the things you like to talk about or see beir discussed on social media. Capture everything from friendships, family life, and dai activities.

After you have collected an extensive list, decide if the conversation is one you woul normally share on social media or not. Write the conversations you will share publical on a T-shirt with a permanent marker. Place the remaining items on small sheets of pap and place in the jar. When the activity is over, have someone wear the shirt.

It is important to understand that social media is public and permanent. Everyone w know and always have access to the information you share, but choosing to keep son things in the jar is wise. Those things can be contained and only those you share wi will know what's inside of the jar.

HERE TO HELP with Tony Evans

Have you ever talked to someone and felt like you weren't heard? You saw their eyes glaze over or could tell that their mind was wandering off. Or when you were done, they just changed the subject? Do you remember how you felt when that happened? It hurts, doesn't it?

Or how about a time when you felt like you had communicated clearly what you were experiencing but the other person just didn't seem to get it. Or, worse yet, they got defensive and started turning the conversation around to defend themselves?

None of those times were times when healthy communication happened. Communication happens when one person speaks or shares information through nonverbal form and the other person understands and responds accordingly. This doesn't mean that other perso has to agree, but that they understand and respond. It's called validating, and it goes a long way i communication. To validate simply means that you recognize the legitimacy of what was communicated. It comes out of a heart of respect for the other person. It is your way of saying that even if you don't agree, you respect that the other person feels the way they feel or views something the way they view it. You respect that they are entitled to their own opinion or perspective.

you do disagree with someone, it's important to start out by validating what they said first. Something as simple as, "I hear you said _____ and that makes you feel _____ and I can understand how you might feel that way." Or "I can't understand how you might feel that way, but I do respect that there is more information I may not know and so I don't want to jump to conclusions and judge you."

Follow up your validation of the other person with what you want to say. Doing this helps you communicate more effectively.

We all know what it's like to get spammed on text messages or on social media from someone we don't want to respond to. Doing that is not a good way of communicating. So when you feel the urge to keep posting or texting when the other person hasn't responded, remember how that makes you feel when it's done to you. And remember that communication is always two-way for it to work. So be patient and wait. And let others know by how you communicate with them that you are a person who brings good to those around you. Let that be your brand.

Also, did you know that nearly 93 percent of all communication is what is called nonverbal communication? Yep. That means you are talking without even talking. You are communicating through the way you talk, sit, stand, what you wear, whether you look people in the eyes or not, your gestures, posture—any number of things. I know, it's a lot to think about, but it is something we all do naturally. The problems arise when we don't pay attention to what we are communicating nonverbally and we become lazy about it. Make sure to pay attention to what you are saying, even when you are not saying anything at all.

Here are some tips for good communication:

1. Make and maintain eye contact when talking with someone.

2. Wear clothes that show you respect yourself and your future; dress with confidence.

3. Sit up straight; slouching indicates a lack of self-control and self-respect.

4. Listen and let the other person finish speaking before you begin.

5. Briefly repeat a one-sentence summary of what the other person said if you need to clarify before moving on.

6. Don't talk too long and dominate any conversation; let there be a balance.

7. Refrain from gossiping, slandering, and putting other people down.
(It is not kind and it actually makes you look insecure.)

8. Don't talk too loud; be mindful of shared space.

9. Put your phone away when talking with someone else.

10. Be aware that if you get a phone call when you are speaking with someone, you don't have to answer the phone. You can call the person back after you finish your conversation.

Tony Evans

UP TO YOU

In all communication, there are three parts. The encoder is the person who wants to say some thing. The message is what's actually said. It's supposed to convey the encoder's intended information and emotion, but it has a life of its own and is easily misinterpreted. The decoder receives and deciphers the message to make sense of it.

If the decoder doesn't understand what was received, no matter how clear we (the encoder) thought we were, we may have to repeat ourselves. If our message is still not understood we sometimes get frustrated at the person listening.

Would you consider yourself a better listener (decoder) or talker (encoder)? Why Give an example.

Why is decoding important in any conversation?

List five ways that you can show you are listening to someone.

1.

2.

3.

4.

5.

Tell me about a time when you didn't feel heard. Do you think there is something you cou have said differently to have been heard? Share what that is.

ead the following story and then respond to the questions:

family is on vacation at a theme park—Mom, Dad, little brother Tim, and big sister Tina.
na—a teenager reluctant to retreat from her friends for a weekend—shuffles along behind her
mily as they navigate throughout the park. Up the ramp and around the corner Tim runs as
races to the mega roller coaster. Mom runs frantically, after Tim yells back to Dad to hurry
ong. However, Dad's not worried about Mom and Tim; he's worried about Tina. She's been
distant, refusing to walk with the family, taking picture after picture, and tweeting away on
er phone. Dad thinks. After all she's almost 15.

e day progressed and Tina seemed to be so disengaged. Later that evening the family
turned to the hotel to turn in for the night, but before they went to bed Tina wanted to share
video. When it began, a slide show commenced with captured pictures, phrases, sound
tes, and songs. It appears that Tina had not been disengaged after all. In fact she was
gaged, but in her own way she had captured the day, key phrases that were from the family
ke of the day, smiles, and action shots. She had even posted them via Facebook and Twitter.
her mind she was engaged; to her parents she was not. What do you make of this?

- Would you say that young people are more likely to be disengaged
  when distracted by cell phones and social media?

- Was it a good thing or bad thing that she experienced her trip differently?

- Would you say overall that she enjoyed herself? Why or why not?

- On a scale of 1 to 10 (1 low and 10 high) how important would you say
  verbal communication is?

- What are some ways social media hinders young people from being
  engaged with others?

- How can you set boundaries to make sure that social media is not a deterrent
  from having healthy relationships?

The boy's Northridge High School basketball team finished the 2015 season as Class 4A sectional champions, but at mid-season no one thought it was going to end that way. The team began with high hopes for a strong season but soon found themselves looking at a 5-6 record. In their last 12 games, the team turned things around.

While they had the talent they needed from the start, they weren't blending together in the right ways. As one of the players themselves put it, "nothing seemed to be working together...shots weren't falling, talk wasn't there. We had to work through all of it."

They began trusting each other to make big plays. Two of the players even sat down and drew up a football-inspired strategy for the team. They looked at what needed to be done to bring the team together. That attitude ended up being critical. Out of their 23 season games, 17 were decided by seven points or less. It was when the team used that kind of high-stakes pressure to come together rather than turn against each other that their season turned around.

There's no way to get to the top alone. You can have a team of 12 talented basketball players but that's not enough to generate wins. Each player has to understand their own strengths and weaknesses as well as the strengths and weaknesses of each of their teammates. You can't have that kind of understanding without communication. The Northridge team had all the raw skills they needed to be champions, but it didn't happen until they came together and built understanding and trust.

Northridge started and ended their season with the same players, but communication transformed them into a completely different team. You can use the tool to turn around difficult or ineffective relationships in your own life.

You can read more about this story online by visiting us here:

go.tonyevans.org/athletes

GAME ON with Jonathan Evans

Basketball is a sport that requires an extreme amount of constant communication as the game is being played. Communicating is a simple concept that carries huge implications through the course of the game. The coach will call plays from the sideline as the point guard is bringing the ball up the floor. The point guard will receive the play from the coach and relay the call aloud to his team as he comes across half court. As the play begins to be executed, the opposing team will begin to communicate as they defend their basket. They will begin to call screens to alert their teammates of an oncoming pick. They will begin to say, "switch switch" when they need to make a change in who they are guarding so that no one will be left wide open. Moreover, if the players are producing an array of bad plays, the coach will proceed to call a timeout so that he can have their undivided attention to communicate the method of getting back in the game. Communication in the game of basketball is essential to having a chance to win.

Communication in life is a simple concept with huge implications. God's Word is a form of communication that, if executed, has enormous effects on the court of life. He calls the plays from heavenly sidelines and it is your job to receive and relay the message. That is, prepare to execute it yourself and relay the message to those who are in your sphere of influence. It's extremely important through communication that everyone is on the same page. However, you don't want to be on just any page. You want to find yourself on the same page with God so that you have an opportunity to win the game of your life. If things ever begin to go awry in life, it may be time to call a timeout. In other words, allow God to have your undivided attention to communicate the method of getting back in the game. Constant communication with God and with others is essential to having a responsible, successful game plan for life.

How do you like to communicate? Why is this method of communication your favorite?

List 3 benefits of social media.

Certain forms of communication are hurtful to people. What are 3 ways you think some forms of communication can hurt someone close to you?

How has communication changed over time?
List some ways communication has changed your life.

Why is communication an important part of being a Christian?

KINGDOM KEY 11

TEAMWORK

OBJECTIVES:

1. You will learn the distinction between unity and uniformity.

2. You will practice working together on a common goal.

3. You will learn how geese teach us a lesson on teamwork.

WORD SKETC

Unity
the state of being in full agreement;
a balanced, pleasing, or suitable
arrangementof parts
Cooperate
to work together; to work with another
person or group to do something
Synergy
the increased effectiveness that results when
two or more people or businesses work
together

*the work or activity of a number of persons
acting together as a team, work done by
several associates with each doing a part b
all subordinating personal prominence to th
efficiency of the whole, see: Unity*

Origin of TEAMWORK: Middle English *unit*
from Anglo-French *unité*, from Latin *unitat-,
unitas*, from *unus* one

First Known Use: 14th century

RULE BOOK

... being diligent to preserve the unity of the Spirit in the bond of peace.   **Ephesians 4:3** (NASB)

It's better to have a partner than go it alone. Share the work, share the wealth. And if one falls down, the other helps, But if there's no one to help, tough!
          Ecclesiastes 4:9-10

I have a serious concern to bring up with you, my friends, using the authority of Jesus, our Master. I'll put it as urgently as I can: You must get along with each

other. You must learn to be considerate of one another, cultivating a life in common.   **1 Corinthians 1:10**

No matter how significant you are, it is only because of what you are a part of. An enormous eye or a gigantic hand wouldn't be a body, but a monster. What we have is one body with many parts, each its proper size and in its proper place. No part is important on its own. Can you imagine Eye telling Hand, "Get lost; I don't need you"? Or, Head telling Foot, "You're fired; your job has been phased out"?   **1 Corinthians 12:19-21**

___TRANSCRIBE
WRITE IN YOUR OWN WORDS

TRANSLATE___
WHAT DOES IT MEAN?

JUST FOR FUN

1. This activity requires more than one person. Have everyone stand next to each other and use something loose to tie each person's hand to the person next to them at the wrist. Choose a task to do together as a group. Once everyone is tied together try making a sandwich, rearranging the furniture in a room, or wrapping a present. In this process, you will discover how each person is part of a larger group of people who must come together in order to accomplish the goal.

2. This activity is known as "Magic Shoes." In the center of the group is an area called the "Pond." The only way each person can get across the pond is by the use of a pair of magic shoes. When the guide taps someone's shoes, they become the "magic shoes." The rules are:

    A. Each person can wear "magic shoes" only once.

    B. The wearer of the "magic shoes" then taps someone else to give them the "magic shoes" when they want to.

    C. You cannot tap shoes that are across the pond.

    D. Everyone must somehow make it across the pond.

Go!

HERE TO HELP with Tony Evans

Everyone has heard the phrase that there is no "I" in team. This is because in all team sports there is never one individual who can determine by their own play the outcome of a game apart from their teammates. No matter how good an individual player is at playing their particular sport, no matter how much desire they have to win, and no matter how hard they work during the game, if their teammates are not involved, that individual will certainly

Experience a loss. Wins and losses in team sports are determined by the strong cohesive effort of the team, not the ability of one individual player.

One of the reasons many people experience so many losses and failures in life is that they do not have people surrounding them that are going in the same direction, hold the same standard of biblical living, and are after the same positive outcomes. Most people try to live life on their own; they try to handle their issues on their own; they want to keep everything to themselves because they think they can handle it. However, what most people don't realize is that life is supposed to be lived as a team. No matter how good an individual thinks they are, no matter how much desire they have, and no matter how hard they work, if their teammates are not involved, that individual will certainly experience failure. These teammates are called accountability partners—people who are in your corner who want to help you reach your full potential. Therefore, your wins and losses in life are determined by the strong cohesive effort of your team, not your own ability as an individual player.

Just like in sports, in life we need to have unity as a team. But there is one very important point we often forget: Unity does not mean uniformity. It does not mean that everyone is alike. Think about your favorite sport or music band. What if everyone who made up the team or band played the same position or instrument and the same notes? That would not be a very good team and the band would not make any music worth listening to. The definition of unity is working together toward a shared purpose. It is not being the same in everything that you do. Each person has to bring their own unique skills and personality to the table—or team—so that the group, as a whole, becomes stronger and advances faster than it would without them.

Again, unity is not uniformity. Be unique! Be an individual! To work as a team means to contribute your uniqueness to the overall goal of God's kingdom, whatever that may be in your particular group, class, missions team, or the like.

Tony Evans

each question, circle the answer that best describes your interactions with others.
en, follow the directions at the end of the activity.

When I work in a group, I listen carefully to what other team members say.

Ⓐ Always　　　　Ⓑ Most of the time　　　　Ⓒ I usually check out　　　　Ⓓ I don't have time for that

I get upset when my team takes credit for my idea or action, and I don't get recognition.

Ⓐ Always　　　　Ⓑ Most of the time　　　　Ⓒ Seldom. It's meeting the goal that matters　　　　Ⓓ Never. My ideas don't matter

If one of my friends is offended, I am offended too.

Ⓐ Always, and I let others know about it　　　　Ⓑ Usually, and I let it affect how I treat the offender　　　　Ⓒ Sometimes, but I try to help them reconcile　　　　Ⓓ Never

If I am in conflict with someone, I make sure to avoid them whenever possible.

Ⓐ Always　　　　Ⓑ Most of the time　　　　Ⓒ I do until I am ready to talk about the issue　　　　Ⓓ Never. I stare them down or let know they were wrong

When I am upset with someone, I tell others about it to make myself feel better.

Ⓐ Yes, especially if I know they will be on my side　　　　Ⓑ Most of the time– I need to let it out　　　　Ⓒ Seldom or only with friends I trust to help me sort it out　　　　Ⓓ Never. I keep things to myself and keep going

When I am upset with someone, I check my attitude before confronting them about it.

Ⓐ Always　　　　Ⓑ Most of the time　　　　Ⓒ Seldom; it's a lot of work to think about it　　　　Ⓓ I am never wrong, and my attitude is justified

If someone wrongs me, I am not satisfied until I have had a chance to get them back.

Ⓐ True, the Bible says "an eye for an eye"　　　　Ⓑ It depends on what they did　　　　Ⓒ Sometimes I feel that way, but they'll get theirs in the end　　　　Ⓓ I try to overlook and move on

I sometimes pretend that things others say or do doesn't bother me, even when my feelings are hurt or I am angry

Ⓐ Yes, I do this often　　　　Ⓑ Yes, with some people　　　　Ⓒ Not really–I like to work it out　　　　Ⓓ It's pretty hard to hurt my feelings

If I am in conflict with someone, I check myself for what responsibility I might have.

Ⓐ Always, conflict takes at least two　　　　Ⓑ Most of the time　　　　Ⓒ Seldom or Never– it is important to tell the other person what they did　　　　Ⓓ Seldom or Never– I avoid conflict at all costs

). It is really important to resolve conflict and be at peace within myself and with others.

Ⓐ Strongly agree　　　　Ⓑ Agree　　　　Ⓒ Disagree　　　　Ⓓ Strongly disagree

PEACE/CONFLICT RESOLUTION SCORING MATRIX

For your answers above, place a dot in the graph to indicate if your response indicates that you respond to conflict using Escape Responses, Attack Responses, or Peacemaking Responses.

QUESTION	ESCAPE RESPONSE	ATTACK RESPONSE	PEACEMAKING RESPONSE
1	C	D	A, B
2	D	A, B	C
3	D	A, B	C
4	A, B	D	C
5	D	A, B	C
6	C	D	A, B
7	C	A, B	D
8	A,B	D	C
9	D	C	A, B
10	C, D	C, D	A, B

Now, total the number of responses you have in each category and enter the number in the blank beside that category in the chart below.

If your score was above 3 in any category, it is time to take a deep look inward and consider your role in conflict with others. Romans 12:17-18 advises us that we should not repay evil for evil, and that whenever possible, as far as it depends upon us, to live at peace with all men. So, we are charged with the task of resolving conflict. On the other hand, while some offenses can be overlooked, others must be reconciled so that we don't harbor anger, pain, guilt, or other emotions that may build up until they reach a boiling point. The following responses to conflict are used with permission from Resolving Everyday Conflict by Ken Sande. Our goal is to be peacemakers.

ESCAPE RESPONSES	PEACEMAKING RESPONSES	ATTACK RESPONSES
Denial	Overlooking minor offenses	Assault
Flight	Reconciling through apology and forgiveness	Litigation (suing)
Suicide (the most extreme escape response)	Negotiation to find a position of compromise	Murder (the most extreme attack response)
	Mediation—having a third, neutral party help the negotiation	
	Arbitration—having a third, neutral party provide a solution that both parties agree to accept	

If you have fallen into habits of escaping or attacking, it will take some discipline to learn to be a peacemaker, but the rewards—inner peace, less stress and frustration, and peace with others—will be well worth it.

BULLYING

The Miami Dolphins were the topic of discussion in the 2013 NFL season. However, the topic was not about football but rather about bullying. Jonathan Martin, one of the offensive linemen for the Miami Dolphins was being harassed by a fellow teammate named Richie Incognito. Richie was using racial slurs and sexual taunts toward Jonathan and his family members that were ugly and uncalled for. While Richie was having fun making his teammates laugh on the outside, his teammate Jonathan was being torn down on the inside. By midseason, Jonathan left the team and went to the authorities about the bullying that was taking place. As you can imagine, the reason for the laughter in the locker room had quickly become the reason for the tension. The Miami Dolphins quickly fell apart that season on the field because of the lack of unity due to bullying in the locker room. Richie's life in the NFL took a downward spiral, because teams aren't interested in bullying, they are interested in unity.

Teamwork can only be accomplished through building others up with encouragement. Sadly, a lot of people get a kick out of poking fun at someone else, threatening them, intimidating them or simply exercising power over others. The problem is, laughs on the outside can be at the expense of tearing someone else down on the inside. Life is a team sport. In some shape, form, or fashion there is always a need for someone else to come alongside and help, encourage, guide, provide, and share in order for anyone to be successful. If this is true, we must always be aware that the person being bullied might just be the person we need. People like to bully others who are weaker than them. Bullying is not a sign of strength. It is a sign of cowardice.

Connor Crisp was never meant to play goalie for the Erie Otters hockey team. He hadn't played the goalie position since he was five. In fact, he hadn't even been on the ice all season long due to a pre-season shoulder surgery. That changed when his team's starting goalie was injured in the first minutes of their game against the Niagra IceDogs. In an unlikely series of events, the backup goalie had also been injured in an earlier game in the weekend.

The Otters only had two choices: choose a third string backup or forfeit. So Conner skated on to the ice for the first time that season and donned a goalie's uniform for the first time in over a decade. During his warm up, he slipped and fell while taking shots earning laughter from the IceDog fans. But, by the end of the game, he only allowed 13 goals on 46 shots. He earned a standing ovation from both teams' fans and was awarded star player. The Otters didn't win that game, but they were the team fans walked away remembering.

Being part of a team is an honor. By accepting the honor, teammates make the choice to win together and to lose together. They are responsible to each other for giving their best effort at every game because it's not just their reputation on the line. The Otters had a choice to face a hard battle as a team or to forfeit.

Without Conner, the Otters could not have competed. Without his team's vote of confidence, Conner would not have achieved the star player award. Connor stepped up for his team and, even though they didn't win, their unity left a lasting impression. While great teamwork doesn't guarantee a winning score board every time, it does guarantee that you and your teammates walk with dignity.

You can read more about this story online by visiting us here:

go.tonyevans.org/athletes

GAME ON with Jonathan Evans

There is not one football game that promotes peace or conflict resolution. The goal of every game in football and of every player is to beat your opponent and wear them down so that you can come out with the higher score and a more favorable outcome. However, in the middle of every game there is another group of individuals whose job it is to make sure that whatever conflicts may arise on the field of play are resolved based on the rules that govern the game. Members of this unique group are called referees or officials. Their job is to not be in the conflict but rather to resolve the conflict, to bring peace—based on the rules they've been given to administer in the middle of the war taking place on the field. While the players are fighting, the officials are ruling. That is, they are the only ones who reside in every football game who have the authority to stop, resolve, and ultimately eradicate negative conflict with one blow of the whistle. Power may reside in the players who are fighting but authority resides in every official who is ruling.

God has called all of His people to be officials on the field of this world. That is, to not be in the conflict but rather to resolve the conflict. Our job is to bring peace to the negative conflicts that take place in our lives based on the rule book we've been given to administer in the middle of the war. The sad reality is most people are choosing to fight instead of choosing to rule. In other words, they spend all of their time trying to tackle the issues of life apart from the rule book of God's Word. Fighting in life without the rule book of life is trying to operate with human power while simultaneously ignoring divine authority. God has designed you to have the authority to rule over your circumstances instead of your circumstances ruling you. Therefore, peace and resolution in the fight of life come only when you take authority as His official. Power may reside in the people who are fighting but authority resides in every person who is ruling.

Are you a team player? Explain your answer.

Do you think that things are easier or harder when you are part of a team?

Do you like to be alone? Explain your answer.

Was Jesus part of a team?

KINGDOM KEY 12

RESPECT

1. You will create a Personal Crest reflecting your values and who you are.

2. You will identify ways you can show respect toward yourself and others.

3. You will create a Report Chart of five things you can start doing to respect yourself and others.

WORD SKETC

Honor
quality treatment that is given to someone or something
Regard
care or concern at a high level for someone or something
Deference
esteem and consideration included in words and actions toward another

An act of *giving particular attention* of high or *special regard.*

Origin of RESPECT: Middle English, from Latir *respectus,* literally, act of looking back

First Known Use: 14th century

RULE BOOK

Treat everyone you meet with dignity. Love your spiritual family. Revere God. Respect the government.   1 Peter 2:17

Love from the center of who you are; don't fake it...Be good friends who love deeply; practice playing second fiddle.   Romans 12:9-10

___TRANSCRIBE
WRITE IN YOUR OWN WORDS

TRANSLATE___
WHAT DOES IT MEAN?

RENDERING Respect involves more than actions; it includes the heart because out of the heart come the actions. It begins with personal self-respect—viewing yourself in the degree of esteem that God does. That moves then to your treatment of, words with, and thoughts toward those around you, all of whom have been made—despite their imperfections—in the reflection of God.

JUST FOR FUN

Personal Crest Activity

Create your own Personal Crest by either drawing it, using your computer or tablet, or cutting and pasting from magazines or newspapers. Think about the things you will include to represent yourself in your family or personal history, as well as who you want to be as an adult. This activity is designed to show respect to your family so try to think of those things that set your family apart in some way: your name, things you do well, etc. It is also meant to show respect to yourself in your future so choose goals that you would like to reach, or character qualities you want to be known for.

In medieval times when a knight was given a specific honor or high respect, his family crest, or coat of arms, was flown throughout the town as a symbol of honor. What do you regard as highly respectable about you?

If you come from a broken home, you may want to create a family crest for how you hope your own future family will one day be. What do you want to be known for?

HERE TO HELP with Tony Evans

When we think of respect or honor, we often think of the person that says "Yes, ma'am" or "Yes, sir." But respect goes a lot deeper than that. In fact, it starts with self-respect. How you view yourself has a lot to do with how you will end up treating others.

Have you ever noticed that the people who seem to talk bad about others the most are the people who are the most insecure? By discovering how to be confident in who you are and the esteem that God gives you as a unique person with a purpose and a goal, you will also be able to treat others with more respect.

My dad "ruined" many a Saturday night during my teen years by reminding me about importance of self-respect. He would do this by telling me when I was about to head out door, "When you are out there tonight, remember that your last name is Evans."

Obviously, I knew my name. He wasn't telling me my name. He was reminding me that name represented something bigger than just me. It stood for honesty, integrity, morality, a dignity in the community. In short, it represented a commitment to Christian living, and my d didn't want me to do anything to jeopardize the testimony of our name.

That reminder always stayed in my mind as I made choices as a teen. And, no, I wasn't perf but I did seek to respect my dad and the value he taught me to put in our name, and I fe inside when I didn't live up to that.

Not every kid in my community was taught those lessons or given that reminder by their d I see the results every year when I go back to Baltimore to visit. Many of my teen friends di early from drugs or ill-fated activities, and many others are still living purposeless lives with li or no direction. But the respect and honor my parents instilled in me helped me to go furth beyond the limitations of the neighborhood.

I was the first to graduate high school. The first to graduate college. The first to get a maste degree, and also a doctorate. I was able to go further because my dad taught me the imp tance of self-respect. When you have self-respect, it pours out into how you treat others as w

Tony Evans

ome practical ways that you know you are respecting yourself and others include:

. Giving value to their opinions and presence

. Not interrupting someone when he or she is talking

. Not being disagreeable just for the sake of disagreeing

. Seeking to understand their perspective, even if it differs from your own

. Dressing in a way that does not cause someone else to stumble (lust, envy, etc)

. Fulfilling your responsibilities in relationship to others (putting your own trash or dishes away, ceping shared living spaces clean, being on time and not making other people wait on you, etting classwork done on time, etc.)

  Not talking too loudly so as to draw attention to yourself

. Being courteous and practicing the use of manners

. Looking at people when they are talking to you rather than looking at your phone or tablet

0. Chewing gum with your mouth closed

1. Being neat in your appearance

2. Not dominating conversations or agendas

3. Offering to give an elderly person your seat

4. Not texting while driving

5. Not consuming harmful and/or illegal things such as alcohol or drugs/smoking

6. Speaking well of yourself and not putting yourself down in conversation

7. Making sure you get enough rest, time to study, and socializing in a balanced way

8. Spending time in God's Word so you grow in wisdom and make good choices

9. Eating healthy and limiting junk food

0. Walking or getting some moderate exercise

espect Chart: Identify 5 ways that were not mentioned that you can begin to show respect ither to yourself or others:

. _____

. _____

. _____

. _____

. _____

UP TO YOU

For each question, circle the answer that best describes your thoughts and opinions about respect.
Then, follow the directions at the end of the activity.

1. I take good care of myself–spirit, sound, and body.

Ⓐ Always   Ⓑ Most of the time   Ⓒ Not really   Ⓓ I say, if it feels good, do it

2. I do not enter into conversations that I consider to be disrespectful.

Ⓐ True   Ⓑ I usually steer clear of those situations   Ⓒ It depends on who is talking and what the topic is   Ⓓ I am not sure what the difference is between a conversation that's disrespectful and one that isn't

3. Respect should be given only when deserved or earned.

Ⓐ Strongly agree –if you respect me, I will respect you   Ⓑ Agree   Ⓒ Disagree– you should act respectful even if you don't feel it   Ⓓ Strongly disagree– all peo deserve respect a tall times

4. I have an adult rold model–parent or otherwise–who treats me with respect.

Ⓐ Yes, I have several   Ⓑ Yes, a few   Ⓒ Yes, I can think of one   Ⓓ No, I don't

5. The atmosphere at my school is respectful toward all people.

Ⓐ Strongly agree   Ⓑ Agree   Ⓒ Disagree   Ⓓ Strongly disagree

6. Treating other people with respect is very important to me.

Ⓐ Always   Ⓑ Most of the time   Ⓒ Sometimes   Ⓓ No, it doesn't matter to me

7. Having others treat me with respect is very important to me.

Ⓐ Always   Ⓑ Most of the time   Ⓒ Sometimes   Ⓓ No, it doesn't matter to me

8. I see nothing wrong with texting or occupying myself with a game while someone is talking to me

Ⓐ True   Ⓑ Most of the time   Ⓒ It depends on who is talking   Ⓓ No, people deserve my ful attention

9. Listening and making eye contact are easy for me.

Ⓐ True   Ⓑ Most of the time   Ⓒ It depends on who I am with   Ⓓ No, I am uncomfortable gi or receiving that much atte

10. My opinion on what is or is not respectful is more important than anyone else's.

Ⓐ Strongly agree   Ⓑ Agree   Ⓒ Disagree   Ⓓ Strongly disagree

RESPECT SCORE CARD

For your answers above, place an "R" in the graph to indicate if your response indicates that your responses show a high, medium, or low sensitivity to respectful behaviors.

QUESTION	HIGH SENSITIVITY	MEDIUM SENSITIVITY	LOW SENSITIVITY
1	A	B	C, D
2	A, B	C	D
3	D	B, C	A
4	A, D	B, C	
5	D	A, B	C
6	A, B	C	D
7	A, B	C	D
8	D		A, B, C
9	A, B	C	D
10	D	C	A, B

Now, total the number of responses you have in each category and enter the number in the blank beside that category in the chart below.

HIGH SENSITIVITY ☐   **MEDIUM SENSITIVITY** ☐   **LOW SENSITIVITY** ☐

Is your score concentrated in any area? If so, it is important to look back at the questions to see where you landed. Does the question address respect toward yourself or toward others?

It is very difficult to respect others if you don't respect yourself. The Bible instructs us to love our neighbors as we love ourselves, giving the assumption there that we "love" ourselves! The Bible also tells us that our bodies are the temple of the Holy Spirit (1 Corinthians 6:19), so we need to take good care of ourselves if we are to house such a precious gift as the Spirit of God! There can be many reasons we don't respect ourselves, but there is no sin, no offense, no shortcoming, no reason under heaven that Jesus did not address through His death and resurrection. He wants you whole and able to respect yourself!

The other side of loving yourself as you love others is the "others." Do your responses to the questions reflect a low esteem for others? Jesus listed loving our neighbor as one of the top two commandments, right after loving God with all that we are. You may be surrounded by disrespect at school or at home, but you can set up boundaries and refuse to engage in disrespectful conversations. Being respectful doesn't mean that we don't talk about shortcomings or problems; what it means is that we discuss things in ways that build up and encourage others. Find an adult in your life who models respectful interactions and make a study of that person. You will likely find a strength and contentedness there that you will want for yourself.

Our media sensationalize disrespect in entertainment and politics with the majority of humor at the expense of someone's dignity or self respect. Now that you have read this, you will be more sensitized to this characteristic of our culture. It is possible to be relevant and funny without reducing your dignity or that of others. You can lead the way.

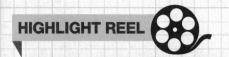
The Gainesville Tornados from Gainesville Texas knew the true meaning of the word underdogs. This basketball team didn't just have a small fan base: they had no fan base. They were an untraditional team from an untraditional school: a juvenile correction facility for felony offenders. Their fellow classmates weren't even allowed to attend their games. The players themselves were only allowed to play as a reward for their good behavior.

A private school, Vanguard, was scheduled to play the Tornados. Two Vanguard players decided it wasn't right for a team to have no one cheering for them. They asked their own fans to root for for Gainesville, and the fans ran with the idea. When Gainesville took the court they discovered a sight they'd never seen before. They had their own fan section, their own cheerleaders, and their own signs rooting them on.

Although half of Vanguard's fans were assigned to Gainesville, the enthusiasm was contagious and the whole crowd found themselves cheering whenever Gainesville scored. At the end of the game, one Gainesville player remarked on just how much this show of support meant by remarking that, "When I'm an old man, I'll still be thinking about this."

By showing the Tornados a sign of respect, the Vanguard students and fans were practicing the Golden Rule to do to others what you would want them to do for you. It would have been easy to make judgements about the Gainesville team based on where they came from. Showing respect allows us to show those around us how God sees them. We are more than the sum of our mistakes. We are forgiven and loved. Respect is one of the best ways to show that.

You can read more about this story online by visiting us here:

go.tonyevans.org/athletes

GAME ON with Jonathan Evans

All professional boxers have one thing in common, one major goal that they all want to achieve. There is a way in which every boxer wants to be perceived and viewed. This goal is sought after with blood, sweat, and tears with every punch, in every ring, and in every match. Every boxing coach raves about it in their corner. Anxiety haunts boxers as they enter the ring and punch for it from their corner. Having it in the world of boxing is a must. What is it? It's RESPECT! In the world of boxing, you either earn it or you don't get it. You start with no respect until you prove yourself worthy to be respected. A boxer must throw the right punches at the right time, hitting the right target on a consistent basis, in order for respect to slowly make its way to their corner. Entitlement earns nothing in the boxing ring. In other words, if a boxer wants respect, he literally has to fight for it.

Respect is a sense of the worth or excellence of a personal quality or ability. Everyone wants to feel as if who they are and what they do is held at a high level of regard and honor amongst associates, peers, and friends. This is a goal that all want to achieve. However, the sad reality in today's world is that people feel entitled to respect instead of earning their respect. You can't throw bad decision punches, always have bad timing, rarely ever hit the target of truth and—most of all—be inconsistent in the spiritual ring of life and expect to receive respect. In other words, you either earn it or you don't get it. Therefore, if you want respect to slowly creep into your corner, you must start by acting like you respect yourself. You may want respect, but in the ring of life, you literally have to fight for it.

Do you think that people in our society show enough respect?

Who do you respect and why?

Q & A

Have you ever been disrespected? How did it make you feel?

Can you explain why this is true or false: I only need to respect people that have earned it.

What are a few ways you can show respect to others?

Visit go.tonyevans.org/athletes to view a clip from
the movie *Woodlawn* that will help you with your **brand.**

THE
PLAYBOOK

LEVEL V

MY NEXT LEVEL

KINGDOM KEY 13

PURPOSE

OBJECTIVES:

1. You will be able to identify your spiritual gifts.

2. You will discover the strengths and weaknesses of your life experiences and how they relate to purpose.

3. You will learn the different ingredients that make up a person's purpose.

Design
to be devised for a specific function or end

Destiny
something to which a person or thing is intended to fulfill

Meaning
the reason something or someone is planned to be

WORD SKETCH:

the aim or goal of a person: what a person is trying to do or become

Origin of PURPOSE: Middle English *purpos,* from Anglo-French, from *purposer* to intend

First Known Use: 14th century

RULE BOOK

I cry out to God Most High, to God who fulfills his purpose for me.
Psalm 57:2 (ESV)

David, after he had served the purpose of God in his own generation, fell asleep.
Acts 13:36 (ESV)

___TRANSCRIBE
WRITE IN YOUR OWN WORDS

TRANSLATE___
WHAT DOES IT MEAN?

RENDERING   Your purpose is the customized life calling God has chosen for you to accomplish in order to bring Him the greatest glory and achieve the maximum expansion of His kingdom. Keep in mind that your purpose isn't just about you. It is about God and how it impacts others.

JUST FOR FUN

1. Choose a favorite dessert and collect the ingredients to bake it together.

Talk about the importance of using the right ingredients and measurements. Discus how using too much baking soda will cause it to be bitter or too much sugar w make it syrupy and too sweet.

2. At the end of today's lesson, we are going to take a spiritual gifts assessment discover your personal gifts. Tell the person or group you are going through th strategy guide with what you think your gifts are before taking the assessment:

How do you think those gifts will help you fulfill your life's purpose?

3. Draw a picture of the trunk of a tree, along with its roots.

A. Under the roots, list what you believe your purpose in life is. Be as vagu as necessary if you do not yet know.

B. Now draw branches on the tree and list what gifts and talents you feel yc have to help you fulfill this purpose.

C. What further things can you do to help develop your talents and skill: Draw leaves on the tree and list those things on the different leaves.

HERE TO HELP with Tony Evans

What if you walked into the kitchen to get a drink out of the refrigerator and it was hot? Or what if you picked up your tablet to watch some YouTube videos and it took you to a gardening channel instead? Or what if you stuck your cup of noodles into the microwave and they immediately froze?

In all of those "what-ifs," there's no doubt you would have been frustrated. Upset. And most likely you would have wondered what went wrong. Is the refrigerator broken? Is the microwave bipolar? Did YouTube get bought out?

If it only happened once, you might shrug it off and go back to using that item again. But if it happened repeatedly, you would probably get rid of the fridge, the microwave and delete the YouTube app on your tablet. You'd do that because none of these things would be carrying out their purpose. The microwave would be carrying out the purpose of a freezer. The fridge would be fulfilling the purpose of the oven. And YouTube? Well, it wouldn't be YouTube anymore.

Guess what? You've also got a purpose. And it's unique to you just like your fingerprints are unique to you. When you try to become someone else, then you are acting like that fridge or microwave. The world doesn't need another one of them; one is enough. What it needs is you living out your purpose. So what are some simple steps to setting you on the right path to purpose? Ask yourself these questions:

Passion

What would I do for free? What would I do for a job even if I wasn't being paid to do it? What ideas and thoughts take up the most space in my mind? What excites me?

Now, when those answers line up with productive things in our society, homes, workplaces, or churches, then pay attention. If you said you could swim laps all day long, then maybe a career as a swim coach or a PE teacher in an area where they have a swim team would be a good idea for you. Your passion is going to be the thing that keeps you going in your purpose when things might otherwise get boring, or there is conflict and struggles. It's critical to helping you feel fulfilled and giving you the tenacity to move forward.

Skills

What am I good at? What do people compliment me on doing? What do people look to me for?

Look for how and where your skills match certain occupations. For example, a skill with numbers lining up could lead to a degree in engineering or accounting. Or maybe you have a skill of bringing comfort to people which could point you in the direction of counseling or psychology or serving in a church. Try to find where both your skills and your passion intersect to see what types of things fall in that category.

Personality

Do I like to be with people, or do I prefer to have some time alone? Am I a go-getter or am more cautious? Do I enjoy leading or following? Do I work easier on tasks by myself or wit other people in groups?

Your personality is a great indicator of what you were designed to do because God has a ready prepared you for His purpose for you. Has He given you a personality that loves to b with people and talk all of the time? If so, then look where those traits line up with differer purposes in life such as teaching, counseling, speaking, or pastoral ministry. Your personali can help you determine what will be the best fit for you long-term in a career and in you relationships.

Background

What have I experienced that is unique? Have I gone through any learning opportunities the have given me a head start on a certain area? How has my home life shaped who I am?

You may have a fairly normal background but even in the most normal of backgrounds, ther are things you have experienced or seen that have made you who you are. It could be that th very stability and normalcy of your background has equipped you for a purpose of bringin stability and normalcy into situations that might not have them, such as counseling or leadinç Look at the experiences you have had to help you understand what God has purposed for yo to do with your life.

When you line up your passion, skills, personality, and background together and see where the link up, you are on your way to discovering your purpose.

Tony Evans

UP TO YOU

All about You

A great way to start discovering your spiritual gifts is to take a test called a Spiritual Gi Inventory. Here's one based on an exam by Focus on the Family counselor Tim Sanford

Work through all seven lists. Mark with an "XX" any statements that seem to fit you we Mark with a single "X" the statements you think may fit you.

Some of the statements have a negative tone. Those don't describe the gift itself but, rath the personality of someone in whom that gift is often found.

hen you've gone through all seven lists, add up the statements you marked on each list and
ter that number at the end of the list. Give yourself one point for each statement, whether you
arked it "XX" or only "X." Next, figure out the approximate percentage of statements marked
 each list.

u'll probably find that one or two lists have more statements marked than do the others. Those
s may indicate your spiritual gift(s). Don't be surprised if more than one list has lots of marks.
u may have what's called a primary gift and a secondary one.

T ONE

___ You're very good at stating the truth, whether speaking or singing it.

___ You're bold when you relate to others—maybe even frightening at times.

___ You talk straight, and your standards are straight.

___ You tend to use Scripture to back up what you say.

___ You often can identify what's evil.

___ You're able to tell a lot about people's motives and character.

___ You want to confront other people's selfishness and stop it.

___ When others say they've changed, you want to see proof—not just words.

___ You're direct, honest, and persuasive.

___ Feelings don't matter as much to you as choices, facts, and truth do.

___ You'd rather confront than just "relate."

___ You tend to be better at talking than listening.

___ You want to proclaim truth and let people know what will happen if they reject it.

___ You don't compromise with sin.

___ You have a strong sense of who you are.

___ You have a strong sense of duty.

___ You're concerned that people respect God and understand His character.

___ You don't particularly care what others think of you.

___ You have strong opinions, and may be stubborn.

___ You're willing to be the "underdog."

___ You can't stand it when people don't practice what they preach.

___ You're more likely to be depressed than light-hearted about life and its problems.

___ **Total number of statements you marked out of 22**

___ **Percentage of statements marked**

LIST TWO

_____ You really want to meet people's physical needs.

_____ You understand the practical needs of individuals and the church.

_____ You can recall people's specific likes and dislikes.

_____ You care about the details of what needs to be done.

_____ You find it hard to say no when something needs to be done.

_____ You tend to get involved in too many things.

_____ In focusing on others' physical needs, you may overlook their deeper needs.

_____ You expect everyone to be as dedicated and energetic as you are.

_____ You want to get the job over with so you can get to the next one.

_____ You want your help to be sincerely appreciated, and can tell when a "thank you" isn't heartfelt.

_____ You're preoccupied with the goal in front of you.

_____ You have a lot of physical stamina.

_____ You're willing to sacrifice, and want to get others to do that, too.

_____ You're often more concerned about getting things done than about getting along with others.

_____ You tend to have a low self-image.

_____ When you run out of time, you're frustrated because you can't do that extra little bit.

_____ You're usually easygoing.

_____ You're loyal.

_____ You listen to others without criticizing them.

_____ You don't talk a lot in public.

_____ You're comfortable with letting others be in charge.

_____ You can put up with people who might irritate others.

_____ **Total number of statements you marked out of 22**

_____ **Percentage of statements marked**

LIST THREE

_____ You're good at communicating in an organized way.

_____ You like helping others to learn.

_____ You insist on using words accurately.

_____ You like arranging facts in a simple way so others can remember them.

_____ You believe that without teaching, the Christian faith would fall apart.

_____ You like to quote the Bible and other sources to support what you say.

____ You tend to be more theoretical than practical.

____ You really love learning and studying.

____ You test the knowledge of those who teach you.

____ You have to know the source before accepting new information.

____ You resist using Bible verses or stories in ways they weren't meant to be used.

____ It's easy for you to become proud of your knowledge and insight.

____ You do your own investigating to find out what's true.

____ If you're teaching, you sometimes rely on your own ability instead of on God's help .

____ You'd rather analyze information than relate to people.

____ You're creative and imaginative.

____ You're more objective (facts, figures) than subjective (feelings).

____ You like researching truth more than presenting it.

____ You're self-disciplined.

____ You explain things with authority.

____ You make decisions based on facts.

____ You tend to talk more than listen.

____ **Total number of statements you marked out of 22**

____ **Percentage of statements marked**

IST FOUR

____ Nearly everything you do is practical.

____ You get painfully bored hearing about theories.

____ You really believe that what's humanly impossible is possible with God.

____ You can visualize what a person could become through God's love.

____ You love having conversations that help you see things in a new way.

____ You tend to see trouble as a chance to grow.

____ You really want your listeners to accept you and to approve of what you say.

____ You like helping others solve their problems.

____ You sometimes quote Bible verses out of context to make your point.

____ You keep trying to make your point as long as others listen.

____ You aren't satisfied until you've shown how to live out a truth in everyday life.

____ It's hard for you to accept failure.

____ You may write off those who cause you to fail.

____ You find success exciting.

____ You tend to give people advice instead of just befriending them.

_____ You tend to care more about getting results than about the other person's felt needs.

_____ You usually find it easy to talk in a group.

_____ You're more impulsive than self-disciplined.

_____ You're able to emotionally identify with others.

_____ You're more subjective (feelings) than objective (facts, figures).

_____ You tend to avoid formal ways of doing things if you don't see the point.

_____ You're motivated by a positive reaction from your audience.

_____ **Total number of statements you marked out of 22**

_____ **Percentage of statements marked**

LIST FIVE

_____ You insist that people follow the rules.

_____ You sometimes make enemies when others think you're "using" people.

_____ You're confident.

_____ You're comfortable being a leader.

_____ You know how to delegate work to others.

_____ You can see the overall picture and long-range goals.

_____ You tend to wait on the sidelines until those in charge turn over the responsibility to you.

_____ You're good at organizing.

_____ You're able to sit quietly and listen before making comments.

_____ You're eager to complete a task quickly and get on to the next one.

_____ You'll put up with criticism from those you work with in order to reach your goal.

_____ You thrive on pressure—the more the better.

_____ You sometimes get so caught up in getting things done that you aren't sensitive to others' feelings.

_____ You like seeing the pieces of a plan come together.

_____ You're tempted to get back at others who treat you badly.

_____ You're good at details.

_____ You're thorough and careful. _____ You make decisions based on facts.

_____ You care more about what's good for the group than you do about your own desires.

_____ You're more composed than nervous.

_____ You tend to accept others based on loyalty or ability to finish a task.

_____ You're more objective (facts, figures) than subjective (feelings).

__ **Total number of statements you marked out of 22**
__ **Percentage of statements marked**

SIX

__ You give regularly and even sacrificially to your church and other ministries, no matter how much money you have.

__ You make wise purchases and investments.

__ You really believe in certain organizations that are trying to serve God.

__ You want to have an active part in any cause to which you give.

__ You carefully examine requests for your money.

__ You want what you give to be of high quality.

__ You refuse to be pressured into giving.

__ You want your giving to motivate others to give.

__ You want to avoid public recognition and give quietly.

__ You want God to lead you in your giving.

__ You get very upset when seeing others waste money.

__ You're happy, even eager, to give.

__ You make do with less in order to give quality to others.

__ You may be good at earning money.

__ You want confirmation by others you trust before giving.

__ Your first thought when people ask for money is often "No."

__ You have a pretty accurate view of yourself.

__ You're more light-hearted than down-hearted.

__ You want people to like you.

__ You're responsible.

__ You love it when your gift is an answer to a person's prayers.

__ You tend to be sympathetic.

__ Total number of statements you marked out of 22
__ Percentage of statements marked

SEVEN

__ You're very sensitive to others' feelings.

__ Your feelings can be easily hurt.

__ You're very interested in people.

_____ You're drawn to people who are in distress.

_____ Healing and prayer are important to you.

_____ You're deeply concerned about people's inner struggles.

_____ You'll go to great lengths to help others.

_____ You find it tough to be firm with others.

_____ You tend to ignore those who don't have obvious needs.

_____ You have a hard time trusting others for fear of being hurt.

_____ You're tender and kind, and often express that by touching.

_____ You sacrifice to lessen others' pain and suffering.

_____ You can tell when you meet a person who's a "kindred spirit."

_____ You're turned off by people who aren't sensitive.

_____ You care more about feelings than facts.

_____ It's easy for you to get discouraged and say, "Poor me."

_____ You're inclined to have a low self-image.

_____ You're patient.

_____ You talk well with people, and they find it easy to talk to you.

_____ You can tell whether others are sincere.

_____ You're more subjective (feelings) than objective (facts, figures).

_____ When it comes to getting along with others, you can put up with a lot.

_____ **Total number of statements you marked out of 22**
_____ **Percentage of statements marked**

DOWN TO EARTH

Take a look at the "All about You" test you just took. Does one list have more marks than th
others? If so, that may be your primary spiritual gift. Does a second list stand out above the remai
ing five? That may be a "secondary" gift.

If no list stands out, look over all the descriptions and see if one seems to fit you better than the res
Keep in mind that other issues, including stress, may block your ability to see a spiritual gift—an
could block a gift from being displayed at all. So be patient, and come back to this exercise late
if necessary.

This test looks for what have been called the "seven motivational gifts" in Romans 12:3-9.

Here they are:

ST ONE: PROPHECY

you have the gift of prophecy, you're probably highly sensitive to sin, to others' motivations, and whether they're okay spiritually. This may not be too noticeable now, but it can become clearer you mature. Being a prophet doesn't mean you have to hear God's audible voice talking to you; means you're able to understand God's message and who needs to hear it.

ST TWO: SERVICE

you have the gift of service, you want to take care of the practical, physical needs of others. u're good at identifying unmet needs and helping church leaders meet them.

ST THREE: TEACHING

ith this gift, you have a passion for the truth and tend to make it clearer for others. You can mmunicate important information as a teacher or coach.

ST FOUR: EXHORTATION

ople with this gift are often seen as the encouragers or cheerleaders of a group. You can bring mfort and counsel to others.

ST FIVE: ADMINISTRATION

you have this gift, you like getting people to work together toward a goal. When you and your ends are planning a major activity, you're likely the one who gets everyone and everything ganized—even if your friends think you're a little bossy in the process.

ST SIX: GIVING

es, this is a real gift—though it often doesn't surface until a person is middle-aged. If you have this ft, you actually enjoy helping other people by giving away your money, possessions, and other sources. If you're secretly wanting this gift in the hope that God will make you rich so you can give art of your money away, you probably don't have this gift.

ST SEVEN: MERCY

he gift of mercy is not "feeling sorry" for people. If you have this gift, you have a strong desire to eal physical and/or emotional wounds. You feel compassion for hurting people, and translate that to actions that show love and relieve suffering.

ther gifts may fall under the seven categories listed here. For example, the gift of hospitality could ll under the headings of either mercy or service. The gift of encouragement might be under the ategory of exhortation.

emember, this is not a scientific test with absolute answers. But it does give you a good starting oint for considering what your spiritual gift(s) may be.

In the fall of 1951, the San Francisco Dons had just finished one of the best seasons in college football history. They were undefeated at 9-0 at the end of the pre-bowl season and were ranked 14th in the AP poll. They were poised for an invitation to one of the major bowl games. Either championship would come with a large financial payoff for the school. This was particularly important because USF football program was woefully underfunded. The future of the team literally hung on a bowl championship.

The Dons were excited, but not surprised, when the invitation to play against Miami in the Orange bowl officially arrived. But the team wasn't prepared for the offer to come with a single, crushing condition; they would have to leave their two African-American players behind. For the Dons, there was no decision to make. What was arguably one of the best team in the country would not enter a bowl game. It was the final nail in the coffin for the USF football program. Without the bowl winnings there simply wasn't enough money to keep the team going.

The Dons' players had a purpose. It's probably safe to guess that most of them assumed it was to make football history. Fortunately for us, they also had deeper insights about who they were and what they cared about beyond the field. When they arrived at a crossroads, they recognized immediately which path would lead to fulfilling their real purpose.

You see, their perfect season was not in vain. The personal victory that the Dons sacrificed in 1951 has been credited as one of the major milestones on the path to future desegregated bowl games. They were simply too talented to not be missed in the bowl season. The news of their decision and why they made it rang loud and long.

You can read more about this story online by visiting us here:
go.tonyevans.org/athletes

In team sports every position on the team has a unique contribution to the team's success. There is a specific assignment that each individual has been given from the coach, based on that individual's size, talent, skill, and ability. Therefore, in order for the team to experience victory, all the individual pieces of the puzzle must be in place. The purpose of the team is to win, and for that to happen, each individual player must take pride in their contribution during the game. The worst thing a player can do is not fulfill their purpose on the field that's been given by the coach. This not only hinders the player from not maximizing their potential, but also negatively affects the entire team. Conversely, a player that goes over and above to fulfill their individual purpose will be contagious to the rest of the team in their quest to winning the game. Every player has been given a purpose. However, winning is not determined by the coach giving purpose to the individual, but rather is determined by the individual's willingness to execute the purpose that's been given.

God has created each individual with a purpose. That is, a unique design that makes them critical to His team. Everyone has been given unique skills, talents, gifts, and abilities which contribute to the purposes that God has for them. Therefore, the worst thing a person can do is miss out on the purpose for which they were created. To be created by God but to never be of any use to His purposes is a tragedy. To not fulfill your design is to not only miss out on your purpose for being put in the game, but to also negatively impact other people that are on the same team. Conversely, striving to fulfill your purpose will give you a sense of accomplishment and will also provide a positive spark for others who have been uniquely created by the same heavenly Coach. God's purposes will be accomplished and God is certain to always win the big game. Therefore, the question is not, Will God accomplish His purposes? The question is, Will you serve your purpose to make an individual contribution to the big win? You have been created for a purpose, and have been placed on the field because who you are is extremely valuable to the game of life. It's time to execute.

Q & A

What role does your background play in your purpose?

Can a person have more than one purpose? Explain.

What things can you do to prepare for your future even if you don't know your purpose?

Do you think a person's purpose has a time limit? Can someone miss their "chance?"

KINGDOM KEY 14

RESILIENCE

1. You will identify areas in your life that need resiliency.

2. You will learn a plan to enable you to be resilient.

3. You will discover the value of not giving up despite what you might have lost.

WORD SKETC

Adaptable
able to change or be changed in order to fit or work better in some situation or for some purpose; able to adapt or be adapted
Lithe
easily bent, graceful
Tenacity
not easily stopped or pulled apart; strong, continuing for a long time, very determined to do something

The ability to become strong, healthy, or successful again after something bad happens OR the ability of something to return to its original shape after it has been pulled, stretched, pressed, bent, etc.

Origin of RESILIENCE: Latin *resilient-*, *resilie* present participle of *resilire* to jump back, recoil, from *re-* + *salire* to leap

First Known Use: 1674

RULE BOOK

Whatever I have, wherever I am, I can make it through anything in the One who makes me who I am.
Philippians 4:13

Blessed is the man who remains steadfast under trial, for when he has stood the test he will receive the crown of life, which God has promised to those who love him.
James 1:12 (ESV)

___TRANSCRIBE
WRITE IN YOUR OWN WORDS

TRANSLATE___
WHAT DOES IT MEAN?

RENDERING   Bouncing back, getting up when knocked down, or changing in order to respond to an environment in the most productive way. The skill of handling and managing life, stress, change, and even disappointments—setbacks—in a positive and constructive way.

JUST FOR FUN

Talk with your guide about how you would respond in each of these situations.

1. Your dad got transferred to a different city and you are going to have to move to a new town in the middle of the school year. Even if you are homeschooled, that means leaving your co-op or church group of friends. You are not looking forward to this move. What are some things you can do to help yourself adjust to it?

2. In class, someone said something in front of the entire class that was not true about you. You didn't have the chance to defend yourself or correct them and now the bell has rung. What will you do?

3. You didn't get a scholarship to the college you were hoping to attend and you don't have enough money to go there on your own. How do you feel about this and what are your next steps toward pursuing your college goals?

List the top 5 areas in your life that are the most difficult for you to handle disappointment in:

1.

2.

3.

4.

5.

Discuss practical things you can do to approach each of these 5 areas with your guide to better prepare you to handle the situation. For example, if you don't handle changes in your plans or schedule well, discuss ways of communicating that need to those around you in order to encourage them to share their plans and schedules with you in enough time for you to adjust to the change.

HERE TO HELP with Tony Evans

Why do you need resilience? Resili But if you didn't have any more "lives" in the game left, it just went poof—game over.

Life isn't a video game, but how you respond to what happens in your life affects how far you can move forward toward reaching your dreams and goals. Consider resilience like those extra "lives" in your video game. It gives you the ability to bounce back and start again.

Have you ever watched a sport like football, basketball, soft-ball, soccer—anything? Any time two teams play against each other, resilience is the key to winning. The team that faces their opposition and responds the best to what is being thrown at them—either on offense or defense —is the team that is going to outplay the other one.

What if someone was playing soccer and another player on the other team came over to try and steal the ball? What if the player with the ball just stood there and let her steal it? Or imagine a football team lining up on defense against the run and the running back decided to go straight at them, instead of weaving and finding a way around or through? Neither of those players would last very long because they didn't possess the skill to respond.

In life, just like in sports, you have to respond. There are going to be bad days. There are going to be negative people. Your parents might move you to a new town. They could change churches, which means a new youth group. Someone who liked you last week may say something negative about you this week. Maybe a class that used to be easy is hard now because you got a new teacher. Or maybe a family member is sick, or your parents got divorced. Or you didn't make the cheerleading squad this year.

Whatever it is—big or small—how you respond to it will determine how well you move forward in life. If you stand there like the soccer player and let the other player steal the ball, you'll eventually be sitting on the bench. When something comes at you and gets in the way of what you were doing that moment, day, week, or in your future plans, respond to it with a resilient mental and physical attitude. Remember, resilience can be learned, but it takes practice. So start now.

Sometimes life isn't fair. Sometimes bad things do happen. Things change. People disappoint you. You disappoint you. When that happens, follow these tips for being resilient:

1. Talk it out.

Find a trusted friend or relative to talk through not only what happened but how you are feeling about what happened. Talk about possible positive ways you can respond or gain a new perspective on it.

2. Find your safe space.

Sometimes it helps just to have a moment where you are in a place where you feel in control. Maybe that's your room, outdoors, in your car—wherever. Determine what this safe space is for you and then go there in those times when life knocks you down so that you can regain your thoughts.

3. Do something small.

Set yourself up for success by doing something small that you know you can do. When you face a challenge, sometimes everything feels overwhelming. So pick something you know you can achieve and do it.

4. Give yourself a break.

We all have setbacks. We all make mistakes. We all get hurt. And we all respond wrongly at times as well. So give yourself a break by not adding on any additional stressors until you have time to think through this challenge.

5. Exercise.

Whether it's just walking, riding your bike, or doing a full workout at the gym, exercise is a great way to process stress, clear your mind, and put you in a position to handle your response to the situation.

6. Help someone else.

One of the best ways to face life's trials is to help someone else who is going through a trial of their own. It gets your focus off of you—and it often gives you a better perspective that your trial may not be as bad as it once seemed. Seeing someone else helped also gives you hope.

7. Learn from it, but don't live in it.

Yes, it hurts. Yes, change is hard. But learn from it; don't live in it. Think about a car. It has a very large glass window in the front. This is for you to see where you are going when you are driving. It also has a very small mirror called the rearview mirror that you can glance in to see where you've been or what's behind you. Live your life like that car. Glance back, but don't stare there. Because just like if you were driving, if you stare at the rearview mirror too long, you will crash. Move forward instead. ence is critical because it makes you stronger and gives you the ability to bounce back from life's problems. Have you ever played a video game where the character either didn't jump high enough, got hit by something thrown at it, ran off of the path, or fell over a cliff? If you were fortunate to have some more "lives" in the game still left, your character probably "poofed" into nothingness and then immediately reappeared, ready to play again.

Tony Evans

UP TO YOU

For each question, circle the letter next to the answer that best reflects the way you think about and respond to challenging situations.

1. I look at mistakes as an opportunity to learn how to do something better.

Ⓐ Always   Ⓑ Most of the time   Ⓒ Sometimes   Ⓓ Rarely

2. I have someone in my life I can count on to encourage me when I am disappointed or challenged.

Ⓐ Yes, there is someone who will help me overcome hardships   Ⓑ Sometimes   Ⓒ Seldom.   Ⓓ Never. It's u me to decide whether or to quit.

3. When circumstances around me are out of my control, I try to stay positive and learn as much as I can from the situation.

Ⓐ Always   Ⓑ Most of the time   Ⓒ Seldom   Ⓓ Never

4. I have experienced trials in my life that I wasn't certain I could overcome.

Ⓐ Yes, many times   Ⓑ Yes, a few times   Ⓒ Seldom   Ⓓ Never

5. If I think change is coming, and it's not my idea, I resist it.

Ⓐ I resist change whether it's my idea or not   Ⓑ Yes, usually   Ⓒ Sometimes   Ⓓ No. Change is exciting.

6. When my plans fall through, I don't know what to do.

Ⓐ Always   Ⓑ Most of the time   Ⓒ Seldom   Ⓓ Never. I go Plan B

7. Sometimes it's good to be flexible, but other times you should stand your ground.

Ⓐ True.   Ⓑ False; you should always be flexible   Ⓒ False; you should always stand your ground

8. If someone wrongs me or hurts my feelings, I can forggive them pretty easily.

Ⓐ Yes, almost always   Ⓑ Yes, sometimes   Ⓒ Yes, but it depends on what they did   Ⓓ Not really; I on protectin myself

9. When something goes wrong, my initial reaction is to look for who is to blame.

Ⓐ Yes, it's important to find out who is responsible   Ⓑ Often. I don't want it to be pinned on me   Ⓒ Seldom. Things go wrong all the time   Ⓓ No. I tend to for solutions the problem

10. I just don't understand why some people will try to do something over and over, even when they

Ⓐ Right! What are they thinking?   Ⓑ Sometimes you need to know when to give up   Ⓒ It makes sense as long as you try different ways   Ⓓ Never give Never, never never.

					POINT TOTAL							POINT TOTAL	
1.	A-5	B-4	C-3	D-2		6.		A-2	B3	C-4	D-5		
2.	A-5	B-4	C-3	D-2		7.		A-5	B-4	C-3	D-2		
3.	A-5	B-4	C-3	D-2		8.		A-5	B-4	C-3	D-2		
4.	A-5	B-4	C-3	D-2		9.		A-2	B3	C-4	D-5		
5.	A-2	B3	C-4	D-5		10.		A-2	B3	C-4	D-5		

TOTAL POINTS

your score was:

0-50: You are probably already reaping the benefits of being resilient. You likely have made stakes but can honestly say you are a better person because of what you learned from them. You ow the value of staying positive and not thinking like a victim. When you don't let your circumstanc- get you down, you gain an authority over your circumstances that causes others to look up to you. ther than blaming others, you are focused on solutions, and you may be embracing change as a w adventure in life.

0-39: Resilience is a valuable character trait that can be developed by pressing on to achieve r goals when times get hard. Resilience requires the willingness to take action, to forgive others who ve hurt us, and to get up, dust ourselves off, and keep moving when we fall. Practicing resilience is eply satisfying to the soul. Keep pressing.

0-29: Whether you are more timid by nature or you have been taught not to take risks, lize that you can play it too safe. Adversity and trials make us stronger; steel is resilient because as been tempered at very high heat, which gives it the strength to endure great stress. Seek esponsible adult—whether a parent or a mentor—who can encourage you to persevere, to forgive, d to keep moving forward when faced with adversity of any kind.

Surfers can tell you that the sensations of surfing go deep into your soul. There is something about being out there in the open water, waiting on a wave, the sound of the currents lapping at your board, sun warm on your back, breeze cool on your face, and the relaxing pull of the water on you and your board as the swells ebb and flow. Bethany Hamilton knows these sensations, but she also knows the terror of having such an idyllic scene destroyed by a man-eating shark that ripped her arm off.

Bethany's story is the ultimate tale of resilience, because Bethany not only got back out in the water, but she learned to surf again—one-armed! Surfing requires strength, agility, and—perhaps above all—balance. Catching a wave requires skillful paddling to keep the board straight and to catch the motion of the wave, but through her determination and tenacity, Bethany achieved what should have been an impossible comeback.

Another important detail about Bethany's story is that her parents, Thomas and Cherilyn, didn't let fear hold them—or their daughter—back from the potential disappointment or the real disability that Bethany faced. Bethany had every excuse to quit, but she pursued her dream of being a professional surfer instead. You can learn more about Bethany in her book, Soul Surfer, also made into a motion picture.

Do: Rent and watch the movie about Bethany Hamilton called "Soul Surfer." Get together with your guide or group to watch it and, afterwards, discuss Bethany's resiliency and what having it allowed her to accomplish.

Thomas Bowlin was born with a disorder called Spina Bifida. The condition prevented his spinal canal and backbone from joining before birth. As a result of his condition, Thomas has always had impaired movement. But none of that stopped him from learning, and falling in love, with every sport he could try. He even learned to hit with a bat in one hand and his crutch in the other.

A surgical error dealt Thomas another blow when he was twelve and found himself confined to a wheelchair. As he grew up, other medical concerns began to worsen. He would frequently suffer from intense headaches and nausea. Still, his passion for athletics never wavered, and he desperately wanted to be part of a team.

Thomas joined a local wheelchair basketball team. He didn't stop there. He found and seized opportunities to play soccer, softball, and hockey in addition to basketball. It wasn't uncommon for him to play a tournament and then have to visit the emergency rooms just days later. Eventually his headaches became constant and so excruciating he was only able to attend 90 days of high school in his freshman and sophomore years.

Finally, a last-ditch surgery, one of over 70 he's now had, relieved Thomas of the headaches. He went right back to the courts and began racking up incredible victories including eight all-conference awards, six defensive player of the year awards, and one national championship with his basketball team. In 2010 he set a Minnesota state record by becoming the first adaptive athlete named the St. Paul Athlete of the Year.

From the outside, Thomas's accomplishments seem impossible. The secret to his success isn't really a secret. Seventy surgeries and years of grueling pain couldn't stand between Thomas and his goals. Because he kept showing up - to games and to the operating table - even when it was hard, he's achieved incredible victories.

You can read more about this story online by visiting us here:

go.tonyevans.org/athletes

GAME ON with Jonathan Evans

The level of commitment that athletes put toward perfecting their craft is simply remarkable. In most sports—starting at the high school level—an athlete has to work extremely hard all year around. This normally includes running, lifting weights, stretching, watching film, practicing game simulation, and studying their position or techniques. This is because athletics tend to demand a high level of commitment to produce a high level of excellence—the assumption being that for every player in every sport, pure talent is not more significant than total commitment. That is, commitment is the seed that must be planted in order for excellence to be harvested. Natural talent is important, but talent without commitment in athletics is like having good soil without a seed in farming. To put it another way, hard work beats talent when talent isn't committed to working hard. In every sport, an individual's or team's commitment is the key to accessing the harvest of excellence.

The goal for every athlete should be to transfer their commitment to sports over to their life off the field. They should remain focused on having an excellent season, but more so to position themselves to experience an excellent life. Achieving excellence will always be hard work. The problem for most athletes is not the willingness to work hard for sport, it is the willingness to work hard for life. The assumption somehow is that sports takes commitment but life will simply work itself out which could not be further from the truth. A strong relationship with God, success in education, and ultimately achieving lifelong dreams are all excellent goals, but excellent goals will always demand the willingness to work for them. Everyone wants the harvest of excellence but not everyone is willing to plant the seeds of commitment. To put it another way, if a person is unwilling to pour the concrete of commitment, they will always be lacking the road to walk toward excellence. It is time that the method for an excellent season becomes the blueprint to achieving an excellent life.

Describe a time that you had to bounce back after being disappointed.

When is it okay to feel disappointed?

True or False: If you want to be resilient, you have to ignore your feelings. Explain your answer.

Visit go.tonyevans.org/athletes to view a clip from
the movie *Woodlawn* that will help you with your **next level.**

KINGDOM KEY 15

GOALS

1. You will learn the difference between short-term and long-term goals.

2. You will set short-term and long-term goals and be held accountable by your guide.

3. You will learn the importance of maximizing your abilities in order to reach your goals.

Dream
a strongly desired goal or purpose
Intention
the thing that you plan to do or achieve; an aim or purpose
Plan
a set of actions that have been thought of as a way to do or achieve something

WORD SKETC

Something that you are trying to do or achie

Origin of GOALS: Middle English gol boundarylimit

First Known Use: 1531

RULE BOOK

Delight yourself in the Lord; and He will give you the desires of your heart. Psalm 37:4 (NASB)	I press on toward the goal for the prize of the upward call of God in Christ Jesus. Philippians 3:14 (NASB)
Careful planning puts you ahead in the long run; hurry and scurry puts you further behind. Proverbs 21:5	But you, be strong and do not lose courage, for there is reward for your work. 2 Chronicles 15:7 (NASB)

___TRANSCRIBE
WRITE IN YOUR OWN WORDS

TRANSLATE___
WHAT DOES IT MEAN?

Specific benchmarks and outcomes you aim to achieve whether they relate to your spiritual life, physical, academic, relational, or any other area.

REACT

Go back to the earlier lesson on Identity and rewrite your tagline and vision statement here:

t this time, do you feel like you need to adjust these at all? If so, write the new ones here:

Read the following scenarios and state what they all have in common:

Tiffani wants to make the cheerleading squad.

David is saving up to buy the latest audio-mixing software for his computer.

Rebekah is trying to get a part-time summer job.

Travis wants to start on the basketball team, instead of warming the bench.

Katina is trying to get an academic college scholarship and acceptance at Dartmouth.

ll five of these teens share this one thing in common: They all five have a goal. List some things that ach could do to work toward their goal.

Tiffani
   a.
   b.
   c.

4. Travis
   a.
   b.
   c.

David
   a.
   b.
   c.

5. Katina
   a.
   b.
   c.

Rebekah
   a.
   b.
   c.

Long-Term and Short-Term Goals Activity (Follow the instructions of your guide.)

ow it's your turn to come up with 3 short-term goals and 3 long-term goals. Write down 3 goals that ou want to take place within the next 12 months and 3 goals to reach after you are 20 years old. Along ith each goal, list 3-5 action steps you can take to reach each one. Sign the contract with your guide so at they can hold you accountable along the way.

PERSONAL GOALS CONTRACT

SHORT TERM GOALS

GOAL 1 ————————————
Step 1. ————————————
Step 2. ————————————
Step 3. ————————————
Step 4. ————————————
Step 5. ————————————

GOAL 2 ————————————
Step 1. ————————————
Step 2. ————————————
Step 3. ————————————
Step 4. ————————————
Step 5. ————————————

GOAL 3 ————————————
Step 1. ————————————
Step 2. ————————————
Step 3. ————————————
Step 4. ————————————
Step 5. ————————————

LONG TERM GOALS

GOAL 1 ————————————
Step 1. ————————————
Step 2. ————————————
Step 3. ————————————
Step 4. ————————————
Step 5. ————————————

GOAL 2 ————————————
Step 1. ————————————
Step 2. ————————————
Step 3. ————————————
Step 4. ————————————
Step 5. ————————————

GOAL 3 ————————————
Step 1. ————————————
Step 2. ————————————
Step 3. ————————————
Step 4. ————————————
Step 5. ————————————

SIGNED: ————————————

WITNESS: ————————————

DATE: ————————————

DATE: ————————————

Goals are the stepping-stones on which you reach your destiny. They are the "how-to's" of the process of getting you to your next level. It's great to have short-term goals, small goals, long-term goals, and large—even lofty—goals. They are what prod you to move forward.

One of the major contributors to establishing your goals is your vision, which is simply your personal view of your future. As a kingdom teen, that vision should be tied to God's purpose and calling on your life and is often discovered by looking at several things such as:

1. Your passion

2. Your gifts

3. Your skills

4. Your past experience

5. Your interests

Oftentimes, these will intersect at a point in your life that brings you to the place where you start to get a vision of why you are here and what you are meant to do and be.

Visions are clear. They involve clarity. When you receive a clear mental picture of where you are going with regard to your destiny, you have received power. There is power in your vision. There is power that comes with knowing and seeing your vision clearly.

This is because when your vision is clear about your future, your decisions that you make in the present will be related to this vision. Either your decisions will be directly related to your vision, or they will be made in an effort to steer you closer to your vision. You will have a clear picture of what to say "yes" to in life and what to say "no" to in life. You will receive the power of having an improved mental attitude about the things you don't want to do or don't enjoy doing because when you know that they relate to the eventual accomplishment of your vision, and view them in that manner, you will have a renewed energy to do them.

A clear vision gives you power to make productive and strategic decisions. It also gives you endurance to carry out what is necessary in order to one day reach your vision. Without a vision, the mundane appears to be mundane. The boring appears to be boring. The meaningless appears to be meaningless. But when you are given the illumination that allows you to see how God is planning to use what you now view as mundane, boring, or meaningless in order to bring you to your vision, you can carry out your tasks with a renewed zest simply because you understand their purpose.

Your vision ought to determine your goals.
And your goals ought to determine your actions.

Here's a helpful tool as you establish your goals. Double-check them against this helpful acronym—**SMART**—to make sure that these are realistic goals and that you are situating yourself in order to best reach them.

S—They need to be **specific**. This will help you make choices on what to do or not to do in order to reach them.

M—They need to be **measurable** in some form or fashion.

A—They need to be **attainable**. For example, don't be like Uncle Rico in "Napoleon Dynamite" who had a goal of throwing a football over "them 'der mountains." Set yourself up for success rather than failure by choosing goals that are attainable.

R—They need to be **relevant**, meaning they should tie in to your personal interests or ambitions; otherwise, you may lose interest over time.

T—They need to have a **time frame** associated with them. This will keep you on track as your pursue your goals and not leave you prone to procrastination.

One goal we can all share is the goal to live a life of excellence—to work as unto the Lord with the highest degree of professionalism, productivity, and skill. It means not settling for a B in a class if you have the ability to get an A. Living a life of excellence results in choices that keep you in school, instead of dropping out. Excellence gives you a long-range view of your life so that in all you do now, you do it to your highest ability, knowing that God's Word promises that your work will not be in vain (2 Chronicles 15:7). Excellence means treating your body with the respect you deserve and staying away from things that can bring you harm. All of these choices—when grouped together—will propel you forward to the next level so that you can live out your vision and achieve your personal goals.

r each question, circle the answer that best describes your personal experience with goal setting.
en tally your score.

In my family, we set goals together.

Ⓐ Yes, and we monitor our progress
Ⓑ Yes, but we don't follow up
Ⓒ We talk about goals sometimes
Ⓓ No, goals are not a topic of conversation

I set long-term goals for myself, including things that may take months or years to accomplish.

Ⓐ Frequently, and I revisit them
Ⓑ Sometimes
Ⓒ Seldom
Ⓓ Very rarely. I live day to day

I set short-term goals for myself, such as things that can be accomplished in a day or less.

Ⓐ Yes, frequently
Ⓑ Yes, especially when I have a project due
Ⓒ Sometimes, but I seldom achieve them
Ⓓ Rarely or never

My goal, when I am faced with a trial, is to:

Ⓐ Learn as much as I can so that I can help others
Ⓑ Navigate safely through it
Ⓒ Find out who is to blame for the situation
Ⓓ I avoid trials at all costs

I have a vision for myself in the future, and I am successful.

Ⓐ Yes, my future is so bright, I need shades
Ⓑ Yes, but I am not sure how to get there
Ⓒ I haven't really thought about my future much
Ⓓ I see only dimly

One of my goals in life is to be a disciple of Christ and reflect His image to others.

Ⓐ Yes, I actively pursue this goal
Ⓑ Yes, I think it is an important goal
Ⓒ I haven't given this much thought as a goal for my life
Ⓓ I don't really have life goals

My goal regarding the role of love in my life is to:

Ⓐ Not be alone
Ⓑ Find someone who loves me and I can love back
Ⓒ Be nice to others
Ⓓ Promote the well-being of others

I can give myself permission to put my goals on pause.

Ⓐ Yes, occasionally I do this
Ⓑ Not really. I like to keep processing through to the goal no matter what
Ⓒ Yes, I do this often – maybe too often
Ⓓ No, if I lay down a goal, I won't pick it up again

Other people set my goals for me, and I achieve them.

Ⓐ Yes, and I learn and grow from the process
Ⓑ Yes, and I am not too excited about it
Ⓒ Seldom or never – I wish they would
Ⓓ They used to, but they have given up on trying to make me do things I don't want to do

My parent(s) support the vision I have for my life.

Ⓐ Strongly agree, and they help me plan and set goals
Ⓑ Agree, they encourage me and we talk about my progress
Ⓒ Disagree, but I have another adult in my life who supports me
Ⓓ Strongly disagree, I really don't have anyone to guide me toward my vision

GOALS SCORE CARD				POINT TOTAL						POINT TOTAL	TOTAL POINTS
1.	A-5	B-4	C-3	D-2		6.	A-5	B-4	C-3	D-2	
2.	A-5	B-4	C-3	D-2		7.	A-2	B3	C-4	D-5	
3.	A-5	B-4	C-3	D-2		8.	A-5	B-4	C-3	D-2	
4.	A-5	B-4	C-3	D-2		9.	A-5	B-4	C-3	D-2	
5.	A-5	B-4	C-3	D-2		10.	A-5	B-4	C-3	D-2	

If your score was:

40-50: You are a goal setter and have already organized a path for your life that can ena you to achieve great things for the kingdom of God. Be grateful that you have a parent or other a in your life who has taught you to set goals, enabled you to have a vision for the future, and wh helping you to accomplish your goals toward that vision. Be sure to stay prayerful and in God's W for changes in direction He may give you along the way.

30-39: Somewhere along the way, you have been taught that goals are important, but may lack the support or the initiative to set goals, self check your progress, and press on toward prize (Philippians 3:14). By making goal setting a higher priority in your life, and by giving t energy, thought, and prayer to discovering your passions and God-given gifts and talents, you find a kingdom purpose for your life that brings you joy and helps you be a blessing to other pec

20-29: There is no time like the present to ask yourself, "Who am I and why am I here?" were made on purpose for a purpose by a loving God who has a plan for your life. That plan unfold as you spend time with Him in prayer and as you begin to serve others. Even if you have lim opportunity to travel outside your neighborhood, take advantage of your school library's Internet nection, the school counselor, or resources at your school to learn about options for your educa career, or calling. Engage in conversations with a teacher, mentor, parent, or grandparent whom admire and trust and who will help you stay on track with short- and long-term goals. When lear to be a goal setter, start small and short-term and then build to the large, long-term goals, and b those long-term goals down into doable, measureable parts. You can do all things through Cl which strengthens you (Philippians 4:13).

No one likes to fail. When a high school basketball player found himself cut from his varsity team, he took it so hard he went home and sobbed. He was one of five brothers who were all brought up with high expectations and a strong drive to succeed. His mother gave him some advice: find a way to prove the coach made a mistake. So, he accepted a spot on the junior varsity team and made sure he was always the first to arrive at practice and the last to leave. He outworked everyone else and held his teammates to the same high standards he held himself. And, his dedication helped transform his team into a true force of talent.

Maybe you've already guessed, but that high schooler was Michael Jordan. Michael's high school days are often told as a story of early failure that gave way to later success.

What's more impressive, and what Michael himself often emphasizes, is that his early high school experience taught him the importance of setting goals.

He always had talent, even the coach that cut him recognized it. But, it was getting cut that motivated him to zero in on exactly what he wanted: to prove that coach wrong. He set a concrete goal of making varsity and worked until he achieved it. Then, he set another goal and another. The rest is sports history.

Lots of junior varsity players probably dream of being world famous athletes, but that's not going to happen for them over night. Dreams are a great starting point, but that's as far as they'll get you on their own.

God wants more for you than just dreams, he wants you to live the life He's dreamed of for you. Goals are the tools you can use to turn a dream into achievable steps. And every journey, no longer how long, is finished one step at a time.

You can read more about this story online by visiting us here:

go.tonyevans.org/athletes

At the beginning of a season, every professional team is starting with the end in mind. That is, every professional baseball team is thinking about the World Series. Every NFL football team is thinking about the Super Bowl. And every NBA basketball team is thinking about the NBA finals. No matter what the sport and no matter what level, every team starts their season with the end of their season in mind. Having that major goal of winning a championship is very important in the world of sports. This is because that major goal controls everything a team does leading up to that point—from how hard they work, to the way they practice, to the amount they study, and ultimately the effort they put forth during each game. The reality is that in every sport each team will always look further than they can see, and diligently take the time every day to making what is just a vision become a permanent reality.

Likewise, the way that every team operates in sports is the same way that every individual should operate in life. Everyone should have a vision, goal, or dream—that is, a person that you envision you will become, a place that you see yourself arriving, or a goal that you envision yourself accomplishing. No matter what it is, everyone should take the time to look further than they can see. Having a vision or goal for the future is critical as it relates to all of your decisions in the present. Therefore, if you find that you are not excelling in the present, it could most certainly be because you have no vision for the future. The passion of the pursuit is always determined by the object being pursued. Taking the time to look further than you can see is the first step to making what is just a vision become your permanent reality.

Q & A

What is the connection between your goals and your purpose?

Are long-term goals more important than short-term goals? Explain.

Q & A

Is it okay or dangerous to have unrealistic goals for yourself? Explain.

Do you think that someone else can set goals for you?

THE PLAYBOOK

APPENDIX

THE ROMANS ROAD

THE ENTRY PATH
TO HEAVEN'S ETERNAL KINGDOM
BY TONY EVANS

THE ROMANS ROAD

How to Make Sure You're on Your Way to Heaven

The outline I'm using is not original. I did not discover it; I simply enlarged upon it. However, I've found it simple to remember and easy to use. It's called the "Romans Road." Quite simply, by using key passages from the book of Romans, we can outline everything a man or woman needs to know in order to receive salvation in Jesus Christ.

Let's begin.

THE PROBLEM

> *... for all have sinned and fall short of the glory of God.*
> Romans 3:23

Salvation is *good news*, but it comes to us against a backdrop of bad news. The bad news is this: We are all sinners. Not one man or woman on planet Earth—past, present, or future—is without sin.

The Greek word for "sin" literally means to "miss the mark." It describes a bowman who drew back his string, released his arrow, but failed to hit the bull's-eye. Similarly, sin involves missing the target. What is the target? The verse we just looked at tells us: "All have sinned and *fall short of the glory of God.*" Sin is falling short of God's glory—His standard.

To help you understand this concept, I must attack a popular myth maintained by the media, the literary community, and sometimes even the church itself. The fable is that sin can be measured by degree. For many of us, criminals seem like big-time sinners, while those of us who tell little white lies are lightweight sinners. It appears logical to believe that those in the county jail have not sinned as seriously as those in the state penitentiary. But sin looks quite different from God's perspective. In Scripture, sin is not measured by degree. Either we fall short of God's glory or we don't. Since the entire sin question pivots on this point, let's make sure we understand our target.

The word "glory" means to put something on display, to show it off. Sin is missing the mark, and the mark is to properly "put God on display." When we view the issue from this perspective, our understanding of sin begins to change. Any time we have ever done anything that did not reveal accurately who and what God is, any time we fail to reflect the character of God, then we have sinned.

The story is told of two men who were exploring an island when, suddenly, a volcano erupted. In moments, the two found themselves surrounded by molten lava. Several feet away was a clearing—and a path to safety. To get there, however, they would have to jump across the river of melted rock. The first gentlemen was an active senior citizen, but hardly an outstanding physical specimen. He ran as fast as he could, took an admirable leap, but traveled only a few feet. He met a swift death in the superheated lava.

The other explorer was a much younger, more virile man in excellent physical condition. In fact, the college record he set in the broad jump had remained unbroken to that day. He put all his energy into his run, jumped with flawless form, and shattered his own college record. Unfortunately, he landed far short of the clearing. Though the younger man clearly outperformed his companion, both wound up equally dead. Survival was so far out of reach that ability became a nonissue.

Degrees of "goodness" may be important when hiring an employee or choosing neighbors. But when the issue is sin, the only standard that matters is God's perfect holiness. The question is not how you measure up against the guy down the street, but how you measure up to God. God's standard is perfect righteousness, and it is a standard that even the best behaved or most morally upright person still cannot reach.

THE PENALTY

Therefore, just as sin entered the world through one man, and death through sin, and in this way death came to all men because all have sinned.
Romans 5:12

Now, as you read this passage, you may be thinking, "If sin entered the world through one man (Adam), it isn't fair to punish the rest of us." Yet, death spread to all men because "all have sinned." We are not punished simply because Adam sinned, but because we inherited Adam's propensity to sin, and have sinned ourselves.

Have you ever noticed that you don't need to teach your children how to sin? Can you imagine sitting down with your child and saying, "Here's how to lie successfully" or "Let me show you how to be selfish"? Those things come naturally.

Let me illustrate this another way. Have you ever seen an apple with a small hole in it? If you do, don't eat it. The presence of the hole suggests that there is a worm in there waiting for you.

Now, most people don't know how the worm managed to take up residence in that apple. They think he was slithering by one day when he decided to bore through the outer skin of the fruit and set up house inside. However, that is not what happens. Worms hatch from larvae dropped on the apple blossom. The blossom becomes a bud and the bud turns into fruit. The apple literally grows up around the unborn worm. The hole is left when the worm hatches and digs his way out.

In the same way, the seed of sin is within each and every one of us at the moment of birth. Though it may take some time before its evidence of sin shows on the surface, it is there and eventually it makes its presence known.

Sin demands a penalty. That penalty, according to Scripture, is death. That means physical death (where the soul is separated from the body) and spiritual death (where the soul is separated from God).

THE PROVISION

But God demonstrates His own love for us in this:
While we were still sinners, Christ died for us.
Romans 5:8

Two very powerful words when put together are "but God." Those words can revolutionize any situation. "My marriage is falling apart. But God..." "My husband abandoned us and my children are out of control. But God ..." "I have no job, no income, and no future. But God..." God can restore any situation. He is bigger and more powerful than any life challenge or any predicament with or resulting from sin.

"I'm a sinner condemned to eternal separation from God. But God ....." Those same words sum up the Good News for each of us. Even while we were still sinners, God proved His love for us by sending Jesus Christ to die in our place.

How amazing that God would love us so deeply. We have certainly done nothing to deserve it. But the amazement deepens when you consider the significance of Jesus' sacrifice on Calvary.

You see, we all have sinned, and not just anybody could die for the penalty of sin. We each have our own price to pay. Whoever would save us must be perfectly sinless.

Two brothers were playing in the woods one summer day when almost without warning, a bee flew down and stung the older brother on the eyelid. He put his hands to his face and fell to the ground in pain. As the younger brother looked on in horror, the bee began buzzing around his head. Terrified, he began screaming, "The bee's going to get me!" The older brother, regaining his composure, said, "What are you talking about? That bee can't hurt you, he's already stung me."

The Bible tells us that this is precisely what happened on Calvary. God loves you so much that He stepped out of heaven in the person of Jesus Christ and took the "stinger of death" in your place on Calvary. Jesus hung on the cross, not for His own sin, but for my sin and yours. Because He is without sin, His death paid the penalty for all of us.

How do we know that Jesus' death on the cross really took care of the sin problem? Because of what happened on that Sunday morning. When Mary Magdalene came to Jesus' tomb that morning, she couldn't find Him. She saw someone and, thinking it was a gardener, she asked Him where the Lord's body had been taken. When the gardener turned and removed His cloak, Mary gasped in amazement. It was Jesus.

In fact, according to 1 Corinthians, over five hundred people personally saw the risen Christ before He ascended into heaven.

I am a Christian today because the tomb is empty. If not for the resurrection, our faith would be empty and useless. As the apostle Paul said, if Jesus were not raised, we should be the most pitied people on earth (1 Corinthians 15:14-17). But the fact is, Jesus is raised. Now what do we do?

THE PARDON

If you confess with your mouth, "Jesus is Lord," and believe in your heart that God raised Him from the dead, you will be saved.

For with your heart that you believe and are justified, and with your mouth that you confess and are saved.
Romans 10:9-10

If good works could save anyone, there would have been no point in Jesus' death. But He knew we couldn't pay sin's price. That's why His sacrifice was vital. In order for His sacrifice to secure our pardon, we must trust in Him for our salvation.

Believing in Jesus means a great deal more than believing about Him. Knowing the facts about His life and death is mere "head knowledge." Believing in Him demands that we put that knowledge to work. It means to trust, to have total confidence, to "rest your case" on Him. Without knowing, you illustrate this concept every time you sit down. The moment you commit your weight to a chair, you have "believed in" that chair to hold you up. Most of us have so much faith in chairs that, despite our weight, we will readily place ourselves down without a second thought.

If a tinge of doubt creeps in, you might steady yourself by grabbing something with your hand or by keeping your legs beneath you, resting only part of your weight on the chair. That's what many people do with salvation. They're reasonably sure that Jesus is who He said He is. However, they "hedge their bet" by putting some of their trust in their efforts at good behavior, their church traditions, or anything else they can do.

You must understand that if you depend on anything beyond Jesus for your salvation, then what you're really saying is that Jesus Christ is not enough.

God is waiting for you to commit the entire weight of your existence to Jesus Christ and what He did on the cross. Your complete eternal destiny must rest upon Him.

You might say, "But my mom was a Christian, and she prayed for me." Praise God. But what about you? Christianity has nothing to do with your heritage. It has nothing to do with the name of the church you attend. It has to do with whether you have placed absolute confidence in the work of Christ alone.

WHERE DO I GO FROM HERE?

Have you ever confessed your sin to God and trusted in Jesus Christ alone for your salvation? If not, there's no better time than right now.

It all begins with a simple prayer. The exact wording isn't important. What matters is your sincerity. Here's an example:

> Dear Jesus, I confess that I am a sinner. I have failed to reflect Your glory and deserve the punishment that results from sin. Jesus, I believe that You are holy and sinless, that You died on the cross at Calvary and rose from the dead to grant salvation. I now place all my confidence in You as my savior. Please forgive me of my sins and grant me eternal life. Thank You for saving me. I want to live my life for You. Amen.

If you prayed that prayer for the first time, I want to welcome you into the family of God. Also, talk with your pastor or a Christian friend. Let them know about your decision so they can encourage you and help you to grow in your newfound faith. You now need to grow spiritually to become an active part of a Bible-teaching local church where you can develop meaningful Christian relationships to maximize your spiritual development.